Elizabeth R. Hill

False Imprisonment of Elizabeth R. Hill

Elizabeth R. Hill

False Imprisonment of Elizabeth R. Hill

ISBN/EAN: 9783744754781

Printed in Europe, USA, Canada, Australia, Japan

Cover: Foto ©ninafisch / pixelio.de

More available books at **www.hansebooks.com**

FALSE IMPRISONMENT

OF

ELIZABETH R. HILL

BY

REV. GABRIEL H. DE BEVOISE,

AND THE SELECTMEN OF NORTH BROOKFIELD, MASS.,

JAN. 5, 1878,

AND INCIDENTS RESULTING THEREFROM TO

FEB. 15, 1881.

PREFACE.

To protest in action against wrong and injustice done to any class or individual is not only a rightful instinct, but is ofttimes a sacred inspiration. And this spirit, this inspiration, should work largely in the minds of all liberal, truth-loving, and law-abiding citizens. Every good man and good woman should do all they can to arouse an agitation against unconstitutional, unrighteous acts which afford pretexts for persecution. United States should be too free a country for its courts, in the nineteenth century, through machination to imprison a lady to screen violators of Statute Law from legal investigation.

SUPPLEMENT

TO SKETCHES AND INCIDENTS IN THE LIFE OF ELIZABETH R. HILL, OF NORTH BROOKFIELD, MASS., HER BIRTHPLACE AND THAT OF HER FATHERS.

Above said book was complete and ready for delivery to the public from the binder on the 29th of December, 1877, which had been somewhat detained on account of my sickness, as I alone wrote and directed everything about said book. I hastened home January 4th, 1878. Through drenching rain and in the baggage wagon I leave 62 Columbia Heights, Brooklyn, for Fulton Ferry, thence to Pier 40, where I am ticketed to Worcester, Mass.; said city I reached 5th inst., 8 o'clock A. M., the train being an hour late from New York.

In that great Union Depot at Worcester, Mass., I buy my railroad ticket for North Brookfield, rechecking and forwarding my trunks to said native place. I then walked up to Main street, Worcester City, to District Attorney Staples' law office, to see and learn what of my law cases (which are referred to in my book) pending in Worcester, Mass., courts, from which by letter or telegram I had been utterly unable to get any information.

On entering said District Attorney's office, bowing, I said : "District Attorney Staples, I have come in to see how my legal cases, pending in your courts, stand, that I may be able to have them legally adjudicated the earliest time, which I have telegraphed and written to you and F. T. Blackmer, Esq., but have never received one word in reply."

Attorney Staples—"This is Mrs. Hill, is it? Mrs. Hill, you must leave my office this minute, or I shall have you arrested."

I said, "What meaneth it?" (Only witness present was Adin Thayer, now Probate Judge, whom I knew well, since my legal association with Gen. Chas. Devens and Hon. Geo. F. Hoar, 1859.)

Attorney Staples repeats—"Mrs. Hill, *leave my office at once,
or you will be arrested.*"

I quietly replied—"You can arrest me as soon as you please.
I am neither a criminal nor a violator of statute law, and wish
in no place or position to evade its legal rights."

District Attorney Staples—"I believe you, Mrs. Hill, but I,
an officer, am obliged thus to address you ; good morning," &c.

I then went to Whalen, monument dealer, whose men had
erected my monument on the 22d of September, 1877, trimming
off branches of an old walnut tree standing upon the grave lot
of Gabriel H. De Bevoise (called Rev.), causing said Gabriel
to maliciously and vindictively seek my imprisonment for
the trimming off said old branches.

The young man was present who trimmed said tree, &c., as
he told me, I had a right. And my complaint as a nuisance had
been given to said Gabriel, and also to the cemetery committee,
within the past twenty-four hours. Said monument man was
summoned to North Brookfield, September 29th, 1877, 10
o'clock A. M., to appear before Chas. E. Jenks, Trial Justice,
as witness of the trimming of the old walnut tree
branches. They did not recognize the black man who aided
him, said justice having received two hours previous a telegram
from me stating where I was, &c. Said telegram I sent to
prevent their searching my house, &c. I had not had any warrant served on me, but told I was to have, &c. The town had
employed counsel (Geo. F. Verry), a lawyer known by repute as
follows in words of Freeman Walker. Verry, counsel, was conclusive proof of the disrepute of the case. Said counsel
arrived ; Town Hall filled, and no victim for the Rev. De Bevoise mob to gloat on. The plaintiffs were wrathful beyond
words at my absence. Remember, reader, no warrant had been
served on or shown me. Neither had I done anything to cause
such a disgraceful scene or act. My monument man said he
believed, by some of those men, from what they said, could
they have reached me, I should have been killed.

And this illegal, outrageous, demoralizing scene was brought
about by the malicious aid of Gabriel H. De Bevoise, who has
preached, as they affirm, the doctrine of Christ, for the sum of
$1,800 a year, in their midst ; and that act and scene of Gabriel
would disgrace the blackest character of any State-prison con-

vict. Gabriel showed himself unscrupulous and relentless, subjecting me to great loss and expense, most cruelly disgrac. ing, and unjustly sent to jail.

When it is realized by this merciless persecution the amount of deception, subterfuge, intrigue, falsehood, and even perjury, to procure my arrest and imprisonment, it will be more than enough to neutralize all the good that has ever been performed from that source.

Report had it at all corners of the street, said notable day, September 29th, at the disappointment of not having the farce court, without warrant, without cause, to publicly blackmail E. R. Hill, all manner of aspersions were floating as to my whereabouts and my smartness, and that the R. R. De Bevoise crew were wreaking with vengeance! John B. Dewing, one of the selectmen, said, "We'll have the laugh last." The crowd went in all directions, when, lo! Mrs. Hill's barn is on fire, to which the mob rush with glee, and say, "I hope to God everything will be burned to the ground. She's 'round somewhere—" [The talk is too black, too damnable for repetition]. Said mob were determined the fire should not be put out. The firemen with the engines and hose could not find water in a reservoir not five rods from said barn, said reservoir being 20 feet across and 30 feet deep, and part property of my own. The next morning, by actual measurement, there was water 15 feet deep in that reservoir. The firemen went some 50 rods west of my residence to another large public reservoir, and, lo! they could not get the hose together right. Reader, do you understand? But the fire extinguisher was worked by one Dennis Cunningham, who, in open violation of orders from some fire officials, played upon the house and barn so effectively, by his rigid determination that the house should not be burned, and thus, by his excessive efforts, was the instrument of Almighty God in saving my dwelling house. And my prayer will ever be to God to repay him more than men can bestow for such an act of duty and justice while surrounded by an infuriated R. R. De Bevoise mob. I had, previous to putting in of five or more tons of hay in July or August, repaired said barn and secured valuable property therein for a few weeks, &c. My hay and valuables were not insured. Nor the rest, one-tenth my loss. Robert Morse, who had been in my employ in getting my hay,

&c., watched that night at its ruins. He said he never felt so bad in his life, nor so lonesome, as if the wicked alone ruled. Trial Justice C. E. Jenks, who obtained his position with two recommendations, had that farce called court of mastery referred to Grand Jury, as I was informed, afterwards, to meet in October, &c. How on earth could he turn over a case to Grand Jury as "Capias" when no warrant had been served on me? Neither had I committed any act under heaven whereby the mob had a right thus to arraign my name, &c. Had my monument man been (the one who cut the branches so they could not despoil my $175 monument by breaking the urn, or its blacking stain, which no method has yet been devised by which said stain can be removed), or had that warrant served on him, I, E. R. Hill, would have defended him in its every issue. But no; they must bring me into public disgrace by fair or foul means. My position of truth, law, statute rights, which I could step by step bring those railroad directors, into public investigation, in the words of District Attorney Staples to Mrs. Charles Kittredge, "Mrs. Hill has joined those directors in every point wherein they have not been in accordance with law, and she can punish them. Those readers who have not read my first book will hardly understand this railroad controversy on my part, &c.

The railroad route was marked out; the straight course would not have injured my land but very little, cutting off a small south-east corner of my land in my lower mowing, and could not have required the building up of a hill in the highway, separating my land, &c. But said route would injure some men not any more than I, but they were directors, and could have sway. I told the surveyors if they took the straightest route through my land I would give all the land taken in my lower mowing, and the corner cut-off. He said he should advise it done, though a longer fill and cut would be required through Kimball's and my sister's and Dr.'s land. But they found the worthless swamp of Kimball most expensive, more than the cut and fill would have been had they taken the straight route.

I objected to Warren Tyler, my brother, John Hill, my brother by marriage, Freeman Walker, an enemy, who were three of the twelve appraisers on the land, five of said twelve being special appraisers. I wrote those men to withdraw their names from appraising my land, as they could not be impartial.

Also wrote to President and Secretary of said railroad company being formed to give me three men out of their twelve, in place of Tyler, Hill and Walker, to appraise my land, and I would abide their decision. Said twelve men gave no notice. I called on them, and verbally and with another letter, praying for three other men, their own choice, in place of the three objected to. They peremptorily refused. I then called for county commissions, and forbade in court their entering my land till appraised as the law directs. This, too, they ignored.

They proceeded to take my land, cut off my drive-ways, filled up the highway, built railroad bed and laid sleepers through my land before those County Commissioners sent one word where they might pass over highway, &c. But came, after all the highway was crossed, built up seven feet high, and, of course, they said all right! They drew their salary just the same as though they had complied with statute requirements. But, woe to the individual who dares expose their actions, &c. Thus you will readily see the necessity of getting up a breeze, and stop Mrs. Hill from exposing their non-compliance with statute law.

In 1636 the inquisitors gave notice to Williams he must go back to England or they should ship him. The inquisitors of 1877 give no notice.

No other cause under heaven but the above parties arranged the taking me off my own land, without warrant or cause, and put me in the vile lock-up. That act was and is a disgrace to every man and woman in that town, and if there is a God He will yet avenge it. Oh, think, that mock trial and fine, with no one but the perjurer, Bothwell, who fabricated his testimony against me. I appealed from that inhuman decision, and my bonds were my brother Moses and John McCombs. I left North Brookfield September 27th, on being informed Warren Tyler was going to imprison me in the morning—which will be referred to again. The 29th I was in Brooklyn writing my book when the farce court was being held and the mob burned my barn. I personally telegraphed from Westminster Hotel, New York, to said Jenks that fatal day. They were far more inhuman than the man who pets a woman and then kills her. But Massachusetts clings to such men with tenacity—such as Bothwell, Hebard, Warren Tyler, Jesse Pomeroy, Stearns K. Abbott, and many others of that peculiar character.

COMMONWEALTH OF MASSACHUSETTS, }
WORCESTER, *ss.* :

At the Superior Court begun and holden at Worcester, within and for the County of Worcester, on the third Monday of October, in the year of our Lord one thousand eight hundred and seventy-seven :

The jurors for the Commonwealth aforesaid, on their oath, present : That Elizabeth R. Hill, of North Brookfield, in said county, on the twenty-second day of September, in the year eighteen hundred and seventy-seven, at North Brookfield, in said county, did wilfully cut, break, mutilate, and injure a certain tree, not her own, of the value of fifty dollars, of the property of the inhabitants of the town of North Brookfield, in their corporate capacity, then and there standing, growing, and being within a certain inclosure for the burial of the dead, situated in said North Brookfield, called by the name of the Walnut Grove Cemetery, said tree then and there in and upon a certain burial lot within said inclosure, to wit, the burial lot used for burial purposes by Gabriel H. DeBevoise, and said inclosure being then and there the property of the inhabitants of the town of North Brookfield, in their corporate capacity.

A true bill.　　ETHAN DAVIS,
Foreman.

H. B. STAPLES,
　　District Attorney.

WORCESTER SUPREME COURT.

OCTOBER TERM, A. D. 1877.

303.—COMMONWEALTH

agst.

ELIZABETH R. HILL.

Returned by Grand Jury.　Filed by order of Court.
　　　　Attest.

WM. T. HARLOW,
Ass't Clerk.

187.—No def's ar' ar', and pleads Not guilty.

What shall I say, or what is due to those twelve men [Grand Jury] in this enlightened, advanced age of the world, where the praises of liberty and justice are prated so loudly?—who are so easily influenced against truth, or dragooned by the man who had been one of the North Brookfield illegal railroad arbiters. Also Mr. C. Kittredge, counsel, and caused their unjust railroad settlement. Said District Attorney was also counsel for J. Duncan and wife, whom I had brought to legal investigation in 1871. I won the case, and said District Attorney had the case I brought against Duncan dropped through the town's interference, and his plea for so doing was: "My time ought to be in the school-room; and he, with citizens of North Brookfield, were not willing to have another court, etc." "But Esq. Staples, they were willing my name should be blackmailed to give J. Duncan chance to get his insurance blanket, and save money to Union Congregational Church." O shame! O Justice, Truth, Liberty, how fallen!

District Attorney Staples knew every rope and how to pull to aid that infuriate R. R. DeBevoise mob! And that jury—oh, shame! to be so terribly influenced, to indict an educated, law-abiding, self-respecting lady a criminal; blackmail her with a crime she never committed, and they knew it! I never cut, broke one stick upon that fifty-year-old walnut tree. My monument man did what he said was legal to be done, and no crime was committed by the monument-man in his trimmings, lawyers affirm, to save my monument. The branches cut would have knocked my urn from that monument, before morning, he said. But Staples as well as the railroad mob knew their only recourse to stop Mrs. Hill was to set two-legged species of manhood that talk instead of bark, to belie and hunt her into jail, as the above warrants affirm. It is an undeniable truth that Massachusetts courts need reforming, especially Worcester county judges, who have, in my case, sacrificed justice to pander to ring and ermine favor. Our judges are simply public servants. They are paid with the people's money; they are placed in the position they occupy to work for the people; and they are as amenable to inspection and criticism from their employers and superiors as any other class of public servants.

A true copy of the warrant I was placed in jail on, January 7th, 1878.

COMMONWEALTH OF MASSACHUSETTS, }
  WORCESTER, *ss.* :

To the sheriffs of our several counties and their respective deputies, and to any constable of said Commonwealth, or any constables of any town in said Commonwealth, greeting :

We command you, that immediately, without delay, you take the body of Elizabeth R. Hill, of North Brookfield, in said county of Worcester, if she be found within your precinct, and her safely keep so that you have her forthwith before our Justice of the Superior Court next to be holden at Worcester within and for our said county of Worcester, on the third Monday of January, A.D. 1878, then and there in our said court to answer upon an indictment found against her for malicious trespass in cutting, breaking, and injuring a certain tree of the value of fifty dollars, the property of the inhabitants of North Brookfield, standing and growing upon a certain inclosure for the burial of the dead, on the twenty-second day of September, A. D. 1877, at North Brookfield, in our said county of Worcester.

Hereof fail not to make return of this writ, with your doings hereon.

> Witness Lincoln F. Brigham, Esq., at Worcester, the 5th day of November, in the year of our Lord one thousand eight hundred and seventy-seven.
>
> > WM. T. HARLOW,
> > *Ass't Clerk.*

COMMONWEALTH OF MASSACHUSETTS, }
  WORCESTER, *ss.* :

By virtue of this warrant I have this day taken the body of the within-named defendant, and have delivered her into the custody of the keeper of the jail in the city of Worcester in the county of Worcester, and have left this warrant with the keeper thereof.

> > SYLVANDER BOTHWELL,
> > *Constable of*
> > North Brookfield,
> > > Mass.

January 7, A.D. 1878.

I will give another Grand Jury indictment before the same District Attorney Staples, six months from the indictment "for the cutting" against lady E. R. Hill. In May, 1876, Thomas Kendrick, hotel keeper at Barre, Mass., was arrested for selling liquor. Said case was given to the Grand Jury, Worcester, Mass. Said Jury fined T. K. $200 and six months' imprisonment. Geo. F. Verry was said T. Kendrick's counsel.

What of that? Why, I was told all T. Kendrick had to do was to go away a few weeks—till *they* were cooled off, and that ended and settled the fine and imprisonment.

That's one specimen how they law it in Worcester County Courts. But the lady, E. R. Hill, had to be forthwith put into jail, and not allowed to pay that marvellous fine of $50 on an old walnut tree; every stick in it would not have brought two dollars. Nor she must not have bail! Reader, can you see how the wire pulls! I will here repeat when Bothwell arrested me at the residence of Chas. Kittredge, North Brookfield. After the reading of that malicious got up warrant, I asked if I could pay the fine therein stated, $50.

B.—"No!"

I then said I would give bail. "Mr. Kittredge, will you go bail for me?"

Kittredge—"Yes. Bothwell says you won't *bail*."

I then said : "Is Warren Tyler going to have his sister imprisoned because the monument men trimmed that *old* tree? Bothwell takes hold of my arm and gives me a jerk. I want you in jail to-night where the town are longing to get you; you will have no bail, no favors from any one." He gives me another jerk towards the carriage. The car whistle sounds.

B.—"There, that train has started; damn it, you've been fussing here; we all meant you should sleep in jail to-night; damn your prisoner all the same."

Bothwell, with driver, turns towards North Brookfield village. On the way he says, "You look sick, but not poor; have you, or how are your cases against the town?" I said, "If you refer to the railroad suit, the papers are all left in New York city." Says Bothwell : "Don't you think it best for you to settle that case?" I replied I had, ever from the taking of my land for railroad bed, been ready, yes anxious to settle, and get legal arbitors from the twelve men, which said railroad company have peremptorily refused. My only offer is what enemies chose to assess." He drives up to Mr. Haston's gate, and says, "I will go in and see if Mr. Haston will keep you prisoner for me until Monday morning at 8 o'clock A. M." Mr. and Mrs. Haston, and Mrs. Pope, my nearest neighbor, west of my residence some twenty rods from my own door. Glad I was to get among friends. And all human kindness could do in that awful hour was done by those kind friends. And cruel indeed it seemed that I could not go to my little sacred cottage home. Soon my trunk was brought into Mr. Haston's kitchen. I was sick and weary, and could hardly keep my eyes open, as I had travelled on boat from New York, and had not much rest the past forty-eight hours. About 9 P. M. Bothwell comes to Mr. Haston's to see if his captive was safe. Oh, reader, can you imagine for a moment the disgust of that household at the treatment I was receiving! Sabbath morning, before I was out of bed, Bothwell calls to see about his captive again, and before bedtime he comes again !

Jan. 7, 1878.—Sylvander Bothwell, constable and falsifier in his statements against me, called at Erasmus Haston's, with carriage to take the captive, E. R. Hill, to jail (whom he had under his vicious custody since January 5, 3:30 P. M.) On reaching the illegal-built railroad depot at North Brookfield, there stood Jim Duncan and Charles Heberd, both faces radiant with glee, with their vile smirk which such known characters alone can make. E. R. Hill a captive as if a criminal, and not one word or act of my own that merited such contumely. I was being held by malefactors to keep their open violation of statute law from being investigated—every point as easily proven as that two and two make four. Arthur Knight, expressman, was not seen even to glance, he looked ashamed as if by instinct. Bothwell was in his glory.

On the train for Worcester jail.—I see *Springfield Republican* has the Bates libel as follows :

"The T. C. Bates way of representing is well known to all who have, in 1874-5-6, heard his falsifying and misrepresentation, as has been thrust into his teeth scores of times in public town meetings, which he now rules with full sway. Mrs. E. R. Hill, of North Brookfield, who is under indictment for disorderly conduct, but failed to appear for trial, was arrested again at East Brookfield, Saturday."

Worcester *Transcript*, Jan. 7, 1878, libels thus:

"Mrs. E. R. Hill, who is under accusation of incendiarism, and who had jumped her bail, was arrested at East Brookfield, Saturday."

Worcester *Spy*, Jan. 7, 1878, libels thus :

" Mrs. E. R. Hill, of North Brookfield, who was accused, several weeks ago, of incendiarism in this town, but who disappeared before the time appointed for her examination, leaving her bondsmen forlorn, was arrested by Constable Bothwell, at East Brookfield, Saturday afternoon, and is not likely to get bail again."

T. C. Bates' ways of stigmatizing exactly !
Where, O God of Justice ! art Thou ?   Where?
The reader sees in the above libels it is stated E. R. Hill is under accusation of incendiarism. Report had it that shouts were heard from said mob at said fire, "Miss Hill burnt it herself." Another: "She's burning this to get up sympathy." And not one man, woman, or child, since September 29, 1877, has been found who could tell who gave utterance to the above shouts. Mr. Daniel Whiting, neighbor, heard the wicked utterances and was aggrieved, working with his might to save my house, and his words were to me since, " Mrs. Hill, God Himself saved your house. That barn so full burned straight toward heaven. No candle ever burned a straighter blaze." Others in anguish at my loss and persecution said, " God is protecting Mrs. Hill in spite of this rabble."

Such violators of statute laws as are concerned in my false imprisonment would restrict the press, the tongue, yes, the thoughts of mankind. Those men have taken malignant vengeance on me because I attempt to examine the actions of servile courts and their violators of justice and the laws. It is to be hoped that the practice of law, especially the wearing of the ermine or sitting in the judge's seat, is not inimical to the spirit of freedom and true liberty. But it is to be regretted that so many who have occupied that position have seemed to drink in the spirit of despotism, and, in the name of the law, vindictive sentences have thus fallen on E. R. Hill, though it has to be done under false pretences and a base pretext to screen violators of law from investigations. I will here relate an instance from English history in 1410. The government made a decree "that whatsoever they were that should read the scriptures in the mother tongue, they should forfeit land, catel, body, lif, and godes from their heyrs forever, and so be condemned for heretykes to God, enemies to the crown, and most arrant traitors to the land." The next year, in one day, thirty-nine persons were first hanged and then burned for thus reading the scriptures (1 St. Tr., 272). In 1541, Sir Philip Parker, knight, of the Shire of Suffolk, in his place in Parliament, had the manhood to speak these noble words in behalf of liberty: "The cries of the people have come to me ; the voice of the whole nation tingles in my ears. 'Tis true, I confess, we have tormented ourselves with daily troubles and vexations, and have been solicitous for the welfare of the commonwealth ; but what have we performed? What have we perfected? Mr. Speaker, excuse my zeal in this case, for my mouth cannot imprison what my mind intends to be let out ; neither can my tongue conceal what my heart desires to promulgate. Behold the Archbishop [Laud], that great incendiary in this kingdom, lies now like a fire-brand raked up in the embers. But if he ever chances to blaze again I am afraid that what heretofore he had but in a spark, he will burn down to the ground in a full flame. Wherefore let us begin, for the kingdom is pregnant with expectation on this point. I confess there are many more delinquents, for the judges and other knights walk *in querpo;* but they are only thunderbolts forged in Canterbury's fire." (2 Parl. Hist., 287.) As a result of Sir Philip's brave words, it is recorded that, soon after they were spoken, six of those corrupt, tyrannical judges were brought to trial. And it is to be hoped that about three centuries later there will be found some "Philip" who will make judges and packed juries and railroad companies subservient to statute laws. Such corrupt, misapplication of the law in imprisoning E. R. Hill, poisons the fountain of society. And sad it is, too, that the chances of redress are so far removed from the people. The judges in our United States Courts are appointed on some political consideration, as a piece of party favoritism, or as a compensation for some menial service they have performed. They are appointed for life, or virtually so. And however unjust may be their rulings and decisions, there is about as much chance of effecting their displacement as there would be of changing the north pole.

The mass of men, busy with their honest work, are not aware what power is left in the hands of judges, wholly irresponsible to the people. And few know how often they violate the laws which they owlishly pretend to administer.

On reaching the jail yard within, walking up to jail, Bothwell turns around before entering the door of the jail, and says : "Mrs. Hill, after I get you recorded, if you will say you will settle your railroad case I will bail you out and take you home with me this P. M." I replied : "The warrant you read me committing me to this jail was for maliciously breaking and cutting a tree, value $50. And you have refused me bail on Saturday, 5th inst.; and also said I could not pay the fine, nor have any favors from any one. This imprisonment Gabriel and the town are making a cat's paw to compel me to surrender my railroad suit as it may please them to adjust."

Bothwell then entered me within the presence of one A. Earle, and says, "This is Mrs. Hill, prisoner." I said, "Yes, prisoner, but not criminal. The criminals are those who are sending me into your custody." A. Earle says, "Be careful what you say here" A. Earle proceeded to take my name, age, height, &c., with evident satisfaction. The matron came to aid me into the large sewing room, and as I was about to go up stairs, Bothwell repeats, "Mrs. Hill, you better do as I told you." I said I was now registered as if a criminal, and here I shall stay to await the meeting of the Grand Jury the 21st inst., as the warrant directs. I will here interpolate on the railroad train down to jail ; there were bonum magnum Nye, George C. Lincoln, and it was also said my brother, Warren Tyler, who was also chairman of the Selectmen. George Lincoln came to me, taking his glove off and extending his hand to me as respectful greeting. I could not have played the part of such a hypocrite. G. C. Lincoln was selectman and Bonum Nye was our railroad president. B. Nye would be thinking and compressing his lips and nodding his head, as if administering the severest tongue chastisement. Which, notwithstanding, all made a point of ludicrous feeling in my woe. He was rehearsing what to say to me, I guess.

E. R. Hill in jail, behind bars, the key turned upon said lady, and ranked with criminals. But martyrs have thus been treated before me.

Miss Goodwin brought me my food on a plate with a cup of tea, and silver knife and fork; also a *bread pan with pudding* and molasses. She smilingly said, "I took this along, as if you were to eat with the rest. But they will be informed your food will be separate." Some of the six women in the other room seemed quite content, but some looked evil, and more—there were three about to leave, and it seemed as if they had been unjustly detained in jail. Sheriff Sprague, of said jail, came up to see me the second day. He seemed very much annoyed at my presence there; he could not see why they had not settled that tree claim. He promised to bring me an English poem to read, but was very anxious I should be bailed out, as it would look better not to go from jail to court. I therefore sent to John Gilman, Samuel Davis, Mr. Cimmons, Wm. Blanchard and Albert Marble to call on me. The three first named came, also my brother Moses; he told me the town, who had arrested me, would not let any one bail me out but the very ones who put me in. I then wrote to Trial Justice Duel, and he came next train, and seemed very glad to see me; but also showed himself in the ring, as he would only say he thought my best course to be to give up or settle all those cases between myself and others. I told him I sent for him to bail me out of jail, on the advice of Sheriff Sprague, and if he was not ready to bail me, the reason why was obvious. He was somewhat chagrined, I think, at my not being so depressed as to surrender all, as Whittlesey did the keys to the North-hampton bank robbers.

My bed Miss Goodwin gave me had cotton pillows and new bed blankets, and my bedstead was an old fashioned high-post bedstead, with very good mattresses. The air was pure in the room, as it was large enough to seat three or four hundred people.

I wrote for Mr. Haston and wife to come down and see me. Mrs. Haston came. Mr. Haston, from what he overheard, he knew they were going to place me somewhere else, and his coming would not avail anything. And I guess he was not quite ready to be made a sacrifice as those were in 1629, who aided any one they sought to condemn.

January 15th I received a letter from New York. A copy I here insert :

NEW YORK, Jan. 14th, 1878.

MRS. HILL:

Proprietor sick, and it is impossible for me to leave. Mrs. W. says do not worry.   Yours, &c.,

E. D. M.

The above said letter was mailed at New York January 14th, 7 P. M., to Mrs. E. R. Hill, Worcester Jail, Worcester, Mass.

Of course all letters are read before given to those addressed. Assistant Earle wanted to know what that letter meant. I told him he had his right to read, but he could not oblige me to interpret. Accordingly he telegraphed to Warren Tyler, and W. T.'s wife told Mr. Haston W. T. did not want anything to do with it. Oh, shame ! Oh, crime of the most fiendish hue is now brought to light !

That letter of E. D. M. caused a great agitation among those conspirators; delay another day was dangerous. They had not my papers, nor could they find out where they were. And only six days more, and Mrs. E. R. Hill could appear before that Grand Jury of the 21st of January, 1878. And that railroad De Bevoise conspiracy, plot, incarcerating, said E. R. Hill in jail, must not have a hearing! Those men would be, if law was enacted, in the same condition of the Scripture Haman. We must dispose of her ; our only recourse now is to get her into a lunatic asylum ; that, that alone will clear our reputation. Yes, this will give us a covering for every theft, blasphemy, perjury, seduction, fornication, free-loveism, comonism. Yes, every violation of statute law—justice, truth, mercy. This is a prime idea ; it must be carried out ; yes, this carried out, will fix E. R. Hill, so we can have no more fear of her bringing us to statute investigation for the above-mentioned specifications. This new plot will end E. R. Hill sure. The jail warden telegraphs to Warren Tyler ; he comes ; brings into jail the free-love confederate, Oramel Martin, and calls for his *sister*, E. R. Hill, and with a quid of tobacco under his tongue, says: " Well, I come down to see if you want me to bail you out." Mrs. Hill: " No, sir. You have aided Gabriel De Bevoise in putting me in this jail, as if a criminal—you cannot bail me out." Free-

love Oramel Martin then says: " Won't you let me bail you out ?"
Mrs. H.: " No; I told you, sir, for your assault upon my person
at the time of my law suit vs. J. Duncan and wife, 1871, never
dare to speak to me again. And you dare, sir, thus to insult me in
this my time of captivity !!' Mrs. Haston, neighbor, who lives
within forty rods of my residence, was at this time calling on
me, and had brought me a change of flannels from my home.
Mrs. Haston was repeatedly asked how I appeared (as she
has since informed me). She said: "As calm and natural as she
ever saw me in her life."

But, reader, the transfer warrant was made out by those men
or conspirators, January 15th, as you will see; and the 16th,
those men, after the papers were made out, came and asked me
to have them bail me out that I might go home. I saw, reader,
the moment my eyes rested on those men, a new plot was to be
figured.

These men did not lure by their false pretext, and neither had
they the first thought of bailing me out. For in less than one
hour from their coming into jail, E. R. Hill was going with two
officers as charged in this most terrible of all perjury warrant in
Hack to that Stone Ark Lunatic Hell. And I will say here, for
fear I may pass it over, that was I, and could I speak, my last
breath would be that such a crazy ark (which holds so many fear-
fully lost species of humanity) ought not to have foundation on
earth. And no cottage ought to have over one dozen crazy
inmates, and those ought to have capable physicians and
nurses, not the weak, simple-minded M.D. and nurses
who are not capable of supporting themselves only in this
modern way. Overturn, and overturn, Almighty God, till such
places are exterminated from the earth. Back to Jubilant T. C.
Bates, Tyler, Martin, Nye Bacheller, War Officers and Judges.
Reporting and rejoicing on that 21st day of January, on the
reading of the cases to be brought before *that Grand Jury and
District Attorney Staples*, when reaching that marvelous, malicious, Gabriel De Bevoise Commonwealth vs. Elizabeth R. Hill,
for " tree cutting." Of course there was a devil, legal lackey,
ready from the plotting plaintiffs to yell. Defendant is in Lunatic Asylum. Is not that—one of the most terrible of crimes—
left so long unpunished, enough to shake the strongest faith in
belief of a God? I say yes, yes. But, oh, I still cling to Him,

that Thou wilt, in Thine own time and way, bring those men to swift retribution. Thou knowest, Almighty God, no savage Indian ever held up the scalp of a white victim with more fiendish exultation, vindictive hatred, and malicious revenge than those above referred to men have manifested towards E. R. Hill, because said E R. H. questions these men in robbing her of her land in violation of the statute. I was not allowed disinterested appraisers. The County Commissioners did not comply with the statutes. Neither had the town of North Brookfield, Mass., any right to sink a debt upon the town on the 29th January, 1875— 5 per cent. of her valuation. When in two days more said town could not be taxed but 3 per cent. of her valuation.

Remember, reader, the money was to be borrowed and all contracts for that debt was to be executed after the 3 per cent. law was statute. And thrusting E. R. Hill in a lock-up *without cause* and without warrant, and let out for two days from said lock-up before they held their farce court, and then their point was illegal, a *Lie.*

That my readers may realize somewhat the fearful perjury of those men in the following warrant, I will state my last born twin babes died in March, 1859. . . . I commenced school-teaching August, 1859, and continued to teach public and private school until September, 1877, in that time instructing over two thousand scholars (and called most efficient teacher), and was then stopped only by the malicious plot of those R. R. men who caused me, for to keep my liberty, to leave my sacred home, 8 P.M., September 27, 1877. Their plot being to imprison me and thus prevent the contesting of my R. R. suit, which is herein stated, those men being R. R. defendants And in no time, or place, or sickness, was I ever demented. Also I wrote obituaries and was newspaper correspondent for the public, and the following my last obituary:

Died, September 20, 1880, of typhoid fever, Lila B. Whiting, aged 23 years 10 months 19 days.

Who can describe the desolation of a home, that unutterable sense of loss which fills our hearts at this sudden death of Miss Whiting, in whose person and character was blended all that was lovely and beautiful. Miss Whiting attended church as usual on the 12th inst., where her harp-like voice has been heard in the choir for a number of years. And her open ingenuous countenance was ever radiant with truth's holy light. But how like a dream it comes to us on the 19th inst.! The dew of death is on her brow! And before the rising of another sun death lies on her, like an untimely frost upon the choicest flower of all the field. When told she had but a few hours to live, she was surprised, and said she had a happy life, and everything to live for, and would like to live; but God's will be done. She leaves a father and two brothers—her mother died December, 1875, and she has since had charge of her father's house, making her home the type of loveliness and purity, all of the works that beautify woman. Teach us to bear Thy chastening wrath, O God! To kiss with quivering lips, to humbly kiss Thy rod. On the cold cheek of death beauty and roses are blended, and beauty immortal awakes from the tomb.

ELIZABETH R. HILL, Sept. 23, 1880.

[COPY.]

ELIZABETH R. HILL.

Jan. 15, A.D. 1878.

NORTH BROOKFIELD, MASS.

(The original is to be left at the Hospital, and a copy thereof and the return thereon
delivered to the Judge who issued it, for allowance of fees.)

COMMONWEALTH OF MASSACHUSETTS.

WORCESTER, *ss.*

> To the Sheriff of our County of Worcester, his
> Deputies, the Constables of Worcester, in said
> County, or Oramel Martin, of Worcester, in said
> County, and to the Superintendent of the Wor-
> cester Lunatic Hospital,

GREETING :

WHEREAS, it hath been made to appear to me, Henry Chapin,
Judge of the Probate Court for the said County of Worcester,
after a full hearing in the matter, that Elizabeth R. Hill, of
North Brookfield, in said county, is an insane person, and a
proper subject for the treatment and custody of said institution.
These are, therefore, in the name of the Commonwealth of Massachusetts, to command you, the said Sheriff, Deputies, Constables, Oramel Martin, and each of you, forthwith to take the said
lunatic, to carry her to the Worcester Lunatic Hospital, aforesaid, and to deliver her to the Superintendent thereof, together
with this precept. And you, the said Superintendent, are hereby
commanded to receive the said lunatic into said Hospital, and
her therein to detain until she shall be discharged therefrom in
due course of law.

Given under my hand this sixteenth day of January, in the
year of our Lord one thousand eight hundred and seventy-
eight.

HENRY CHAPIN,
Judge of Probate Court.

WORCESTER, *ss.*   January 16, 1878.

I hereby certify that the above-named Elizabeth R. Hill, is now resident in North Brookfield, in the County of Worcester.

HENRY CHAPIN,
Judge of Probate Court.

COMMONWEALTH OF MASSACHUSETTS.

WORCESTER, *ss.*

In obedience to the foregoing warrant, I have taken and delivered the within named Elizabeth R. Hill to the Superintendent of the Worcester Lunatic Hospital, together with this warrant and the annexed statement of particulars concerning her.

I certify that the extra charge on this warrant was actually and necessarily incurred and disbursed, and is reasonable.

JAS. M. DRENNAN,
Deputy Sheriff.

Fees—Service,
       Travel,
       Copy,

WORCESTER, *ss.*   A. D. 187

Personally appeared
and made oath that the foregoing statement, by him subscribed, is true.

       Before me,

Justice of the Peace.

NAMES OF PHYSICIANS.

ORAMEL MARTIN,
Worcester.

WARREN TYLER,
North Brookfield.

24

(Copy of Statement filed by Applicant.)

To the Honorable Judge of the Probate Court in and for the County of Worcester:

The subscriber, having made application to your Honor for the commitment of Elizabeth R. Hill to the Worcester Lunatic Hospital as a lunatic, now presents the following statement in answer to interrogatories :

What is the age of the lunatic?   Ans. About forty-eight years.

Birthplace?   Ans. North Brookfield.

Married?   Ans. Widow.

Occupation?   Ans. School Teacher.

Supposed cause of disease?   Ans. Family troubles.

Duration?   Ans. Twenty years.

Character—whether mild, violent, or dangerous?   Ans. Dangerous.

Homicidal or suicidal?   Ans. Homicidal.

Paralytic or epileptic?   Ans. No.

Previous existence of insanity in the lunatic?   Ans. No.

Previous or present insanity in any of the family?   Ans. No.

Habits in regard to temperance?   Ans. Temperate.

Whether she has been in any lunatic hospital ; if so, what one, when, and how long?   Ans. No.

{ (If a woman.)
Has she ever borne any children?   Ans. Yes.
How long since the birth of her last child?   Ans. Twenty-eight years.

Name and Post Office address of some one of the nearest relatives or friends?   Ans. Erasmus Haston, North Brookfield.

What facts show whether she has or has not a settlement, and where, if anywhere in this State?   Ans. North Brookfield; and has owned property, and paid taxes there.

(For the law relating to settlement, see Gen. Stat.. chap. 09.
Supplement to Gen. Stat., 1863. chap 328.
do.   do.   1870,   "   392.
do.   do.   1871,   "   379.
do.   do.   1874,   "   274.)

BRO. DR. WARREN TYLER, No. Brookfield.

Copy—Attest,

ORAMEL MARTIN,
Applicant.

HENRY CHAPIN,
Judge.

SKETCHES AND THOUGHTS IN THE LIFE OF ELIZABETH R. HILL.

WRITTEN BEHIND LUNATIC BARS AND BOLTS IN WORCESTER, MASS.

January, 1878.

E. R. HILL has been indicted by North Brookfield railroad. De Bevoise mob blackmailed me through all papers; fired my buildings; and when I returned from New York, January 5, 1878, to meet each and every charge of said mob, as the statutes direct, said mob, ere I could reach my home, I was placed in jail on a *capias* warrant, issued by Gabriel H. De Bevoise, through the catspaw, the Town (North Brookfield, Mass.), said warrant being defective, as said E. R. Hill had never been arrested on said warrant before said E. R. demanded release from said jail because of said defect in said warrant. Sheriff Sprague, of said jail, and Court, seeing their net had caught said mob in its meshes, therefore said body, as their only recourse, turned said prosecution, by the perjury of Oramel Martin and Warren Tyler and said sheriff, by statute chicanery into persecution, and by said chicanery caused said E. R. Hill to be transferred to the Stone-Ark lunatic asylum in Worcester, Mass., thus hoping through a machination to end or crush out the life of said E. R. Hill, and thus prevent investigation of their violation of the statutes in firing my buildings, in their press blackmail, the De Bevoise plot and intrigue to aid the North Brookfield railroad mob out, if possible, of this fearful imprisonment, illegal offences fully set forth in my book issued Dec. 29, 1877 (Sketches and Incidents in the Life of E. R. Hill), thus showing said Gabriel to be ten times more a child of hell than the rest of said mob! Turnkey Wilson of said jail and said Masons had two newspaper reporters to witness this crime, and two other men. Thus I was viewed in jail by four tool-men, hoping to gather some newspaper-hell report. The awful look-devil, indeed, of said Wilson; the taunt of A. Earle in his jubilant good-bye made an impress as with a red-hot iron on my educated, sensitive mind. Miss Goodwin, matron, had a tear of surprised sympathy in her eyes, and the Irish woman in jail for some trivial offence stood aghast with dismay, saying, "Why, how awful!" when said E.

R. Hill told them, instead of going to my home, I was being sent to an insane asylum. " Oh, oh, oh !" they all exclaimed ; and my dismay was unbounded.

At this hospital, second day, Drs. Eastman and Quimby came into my room. I tried to tell them why I was here, etc. Eastman said I had been sent by the Court here as insane, and they were to find out so and so.

Then a ray of hope shot into my dismayed soul, perchance a human spark of truth might rest in them that plot nor money could not buy. Thus time has worn on till that hope has sunk to despair. I am fully convinced I am sold as much as ever Joseph, or Christ, or John Brown, John Rogers, or Abraham Lincoln was given up as martyrs for reform. But, O God, let this cup pass if it can be Thy holy will, and return me to my loved sacred home and that of my fathers. Thou knowest me altogether. Thou knowest I love and fear Thee, and hast ever kept Thy commandments, Thou Deity, who holdest all within Thy mighty fists, I pray Thee break said mob's straws and melt away their mists !

ELIZABETH R. HILL.

THOUGHTS.

January, 1878.

I HAVE to endure, because in this prison I am powerless to have things otherwise.

Oh, could I secure an atmosphere of quiet from this maniac rabble ! it is more torturing than a scorpion's whip !

WORCESTER HOSPITAL, Feb. 1, 1878.

Mrs. —— ——, N. Y. City :

Dear Friend—I wrote you from jail, and duly received reply. Was arrested on Saturday, 5th ult., and jailed 7th ult. Mr. Haston, my neighbor, said I should be home in the afternoon, as we understood the reading of the warrant ; but the railroad, De Bevoise plot made a net for me like the " Haman gallows." I hope you will clearly see how my name is blackmailed in the *Spy* and other Massachusetts periodicals. Monday, 7th ult., notice the *Spy* how it uses my name, read it. The bonds there spoken of were the bonds given Sept. 14. Said case I telegraphed to Staples, October 8; also wrote Staples two letters. You also remember about my telegram and letters to F. T. Blackmer, Esq., and my joy on seeing him on Broadway, Nov. 1877—his promise to inform me and put over my law cases if they could be, etc. You cannot fail to see the plot of the rings to cover their malpractices of the statutes.

I did not tell in New York my brother (Dr. Tyler) had never, with his wife, been into my house since my father's death, 1864.

Fifty would count every word and bow of his wife to me. A most common-brained woman, of very poor birth. The doctor has not spoken to me or nodded since my ball-club sickness, 1872, when he wished me to sue the town for damages, and I would not. Half a dozen nods and words every word he has spoken. But, on the 16th ulto., he with his confederate, the vile perjurer, free-lover, spiritualist, low-mouthed Oramel Martin, came and called for me in jail, asked me if I wanted bail. I replied, not from them, telling them the defect in the warrant, and demanding my release from my imprisonment. They, in less than five minutes, left, and in a short time I was sent for on the warrant of transfer to this maniac dwelling! I was horror-stricken, and to the outrage I submitted as quietly as my temperament would permit, I guess. Oh, tongue nor pen can describe the terrible, the cutting disgust and mortification to be sent here and treated as if insane! But, oh, God's arms are underneath, sustaining me in this awful trial! But, oh, how long, how long!

The ten dollars you loaned me to have been paid Jan. 19, or before, would have been paid as I wrote you in my letter at jail, after Jan. 21, the soonest time, had it not been for this transfer. But you will see the die-cutter and the man I owe $47.50, and tell him I trust in God's time, not mine, he will have every cent from me. Let him read this letter. And I pray God if I live to be released from this false imprisonment, I shall find that the parties who hold my valuable collaterals, though the time—one week—expires, and I am prison-bound and cannot redeem—which the parties must know—my trunk, my house, my all, except what is in New York, are in the hands of the railroad, De Bevoise mob! Tell them never to give up one paper unless I call for them personally ; if I do not, to carry out to the fullest extent of the law, and spread the wrongs and outrage set forth in my books, and all they can gather, as before promised. This malpractice of law, the criminal proceedings against me, to cover the North Brookfield mob crimes, and their determination not to let me vindicate one point they blackmail me with exceeds any brutality or violation of the statutes ever known upon record. My eye of faith dims constantly—that ever I shall be released. That Massachusetts, Worcester county, I believe in my heart, is, and will prove herself, capable as enactor of the most savage abuses and blackmail of any place upon the western continent!

I think George F. Hoar, who has become one of the Women Suffragists, would do well to look at his Worcester home, and see and know the brutality, the incendiarism, the perjury of the men and the women who uphold and give, or aid in giving, him his Senatorship. I once respected him; but his new issue—Women Suffragists, his modern consequence, his vote for President, lowers him in my eyes. I think he had better study the crimes of his crew, who are and have taken my liberty, my hard earnings from me. But I believe he would not have the violations of the statutes of the Worcester Superior Court investigated, nor my false imprisonment made known to Washington, were it to save my life.

The doctors must know I am not insane; and, if they can be bought with a price, I shall have to die here. Come and see.

E. R. HILL.

WORCESTER HOSPITAL, Feb. 4th, 1878.

Mrs. ——.—I herewith send you a true copy of a letter I wrote the 3d inst. to the Trustees, Doctors, &c., of this "maniac hell." Thus, if through intrigue, I am kept in this terrible ——, you can know something of me.

Gentlemen :—As the time nears a close when I must be loser of hundreds of dollars by this imprisonment of me (E. R. Hill) by my brother, &c. Gentlemen, this Sabbath morn I again appeal to you as those who will hear, direct and guide me in this my great need. First, do give me a chance to redeem my collaterals that are held redeemable; time expires February 8th, 1878. True I have said, and still say, if I am to be squelched here from my own home, so hard earned and faithfully kept, every spot sacred with associations; if I cannot have and go to my own home, let it be lost ; there is more left than I wish there was. But, gentlemen, you cannot fail to see the Court proceeding. My warrant placing me in jail was a " Capias." I demanded a release from said place on the ground of Sheriff Sprague saying, " said warrant was capias from the one my bonds (Moses Tyler) was sued on." I told said Sprague the case I was imprisoned on was the De Bevoise tree case, and I had never been arrested on that before (a very unwise move of mine to explain and ask to be released, but my frank nature led me here). Sheriff Sprague " was disturbed greatly, and did not, could not understand," &c. Gentlemen, if I did wrong in demanding release on account of defective warrant, will you please find out the truth, and give me a chance to ask forgivness if in the wrong ! Again, if I was legally imprisoned to await the hearing before the Grand Jury the 21st ult., why did they not permit me the human statute right to have that hearing, &c. I am and was, and ever have been, ready to meet said case, and, if a violator of the law, to be held amenable to its statute requirements. But to be deprived of said right by the persecutors and thrust into a " maniac hell," or hospital, exceeds any picture I ever read about. Gentlemen, you must know I have reason to distrust men, though I may in so doing misjudge, &c. My brother Moses told me " I had got to be got out of jail by those who put me in." Have Worcester courts become so corrupt since the war that anarchy reigns to be satiated on the widow and fatherless to cover their own misapplications of the law ? Again, my brother Moses told me " Luther De Land told him I fired my buildings." [Mrs. Haston says, " Don't report anything so foolish."] Is it, sirs, a pass over duty to be thus *blackmailed by evil doers* or their confederates in crime, and have your property destroyed by them ? Am I wrong in demanding said Luther be held amenable to statute laws for said " blackmail," &c. ? My policy of $165, when collected, is not one-tenth my loss by that incendiary fire, say nothing of the irreparable loss that ever will make the tears flow till time is no more. Still add this woe—all I have, my hard earnings, and that of my father and mother ; all my tokens of the loved lost, I have kept, and never wasted, nor wronged any one, are now in custody of my deadly enemies, whose sins will be found out in God's time. " When John

Brown struck the upas branch above our orange bloom, Columbia's wrath, in avalanche, scoops out his lonely tomb !" Again, the terrible blackmail, the compounding of different falsifications upon my name, heralded by different papers in this city (the place of this maniac hell), that holds the martyr, E. R. Hill, captive from everything but God—thus giving those culprits power over innocence and truth. The only way, the only chance, to save their plotting intrigue from statute punishment. Again, the appealed case of September 14th, 1878. Said case had a farce trial said day. The only person at said trial criminating me was the State-prison criminal himself, Bothwell, who fabricated the testimony he uttered against me to cover their plot, and his savage outrage of law, of humanity, and truth. Why did not District Attorney Staples, when telegraphed to to put over my appealed case, October 8, 1877 (by E. R. Hill), telegraph back to have me sent home at once, &c., or telegraph and find my place of abode, instead of the blackmail sent out by the press. My every hour from the time I left my abode, September 27th, 1877, to January 7th, 1878, I can prove to you or the Court by witnesses of my presence. Will you, gentlemen, find out why I can not have human rights and laws that Massachusetts brags so much over. Again, the Court (Dr. Eastman repeats) says " I am insane." Yes, gentlemen, and it belongs to you without delay to denounce that Court proceeding before God and man, and give me my right, my liberty; and instruct me what counsel to employ in *Boston* to investigate why those crimes held up against me " *can't* " be tried as law directs. Will you not, gentlemen, investigate and act as you would for yourselves? Please answer each and every issue herein stated.

When Fremont freed on Western plains
   A few from servile thrall,
One welded, then, the broken chains,
   Who after broke them all.

Oh, God, from marshes lone and wild
   Thy rivers seek the sea ;
So prayers from Thy poor wayward child
   Would find their way to Thee.

ELIZABETH R. HILL.

This is the nineteenth day in this terrible place. } E. R. H.

WORCESTER HOSPITAL, Feb. 9th, 1879.

Gentlemen :—As there is a prospect of sending you this by some one leaving this maniac hell, I write : Do keep all books safe ; box up, and, also, if you have a chance to sell any, do so. You must know, ere this, I was thrust here the 16th ult. to prevent my having a chance to sue the town N. B. for false imprisonment. Will you send one of my books, also the copy of warrant and letter, which I have enclosed to Esq. ——. Tell him my case the best you can, for I have no chance to write him. You engage him for me to enter a writ for my release from this insane retreat. The doctors say they can't send me home till the Court pleases, &c. Drs. Tyler and Martin, upon three minutes in my presence (because I would not have them bail me out of my false imprisonment), appeared before the *Probate Court*, and told said Judge to transfer me here. N. B. De B. were caught in their own net by defect in warrant, making this their only recourse. I wish Esq. —— to write me here at once and tell me what course to pursue, if he can not attend to it at once. Have him send me his partner in business, or whoever he chooses, to aid me from this De Bevoise pit. His retainer he can secure. Tell him my fearful situation, and that the railroad De Bevoise men mean to squelch me for life by this move. But I bear it most heroically, equal to " St. Paul," I guess, but it's terrible. Spread this news all you can ; tell ——, of the railroad papers, if you think best. But I adjure you never give them, or any of my effects, except through my directions ; but do as you would have one do by a sister, mother, &c. See —— if you can. Oh, cannot some of you come here and get me out of this prison. Tell the " die cutter " about me, and the printers ; tell them not to give up anything, but keep till I call, or they know I am dead. And I pray you all to spread this outrage, which exceeds anything on record during the war, before or since. " When John Brown struck the upas branch above the orange bloom, Columbia's wrath, in avalanche, scooped out his tomb." It's just my case with that North Brookfield Railroad De Bevoise mob. And then for them to get me again imprisoned illegally made their position precarious, even having only a woman alone for defendant. . . .

I should like to have my books sent to some of the

most notable libraries. Can you not find out where to send them ; where this terrible wrong can be heralded and shown up—Worcester County barbarism. Tell all that know me friendly to write or send me a paper. I wish you would send some books to the Southern senators, that they may be able to confront Hoar with his own city home, worse than any slave's brutality, to a widow and orphan. I left a book to be sent to the *Sun* office. I hope they have received it. I talk to you as if you had nothing to do but see to this affair. A stranger, as you are, almost. But, oh, is this not co-equal with the murder of Abraham Lincoln and other martyrs? Thus I write, hoping all that know me in New York, &c., will unite in spreading this outrage, and thus bring also help to release the captive prisoner, E. R. Hill. Would to God my trunk had been left in New York. My agony thinking of what is in it ; and my house, all in the hands of my deadly enemies. Those who would do are afraid to move. Mr. Haston, my neighbor, would be bail, but he is afraid; he has property, and knows how mine was destroyed. That Staples referred to did not put over my case (book). Blackmer, you will remember, who was going to attend to my cases (I met on Broadway), from Worcester, he, too, did nothing, notwithstanding my letters and telegrams to him from New York. Thus you see my condition. Oh, may God raise up some one to help.   E. R. Hill.

———

Feb. 9th, 1878.

Blaine, when complimented by a friend on his handling of Hoar and Dawes, replied : "Oh, it's an easy matter to surprise two old women."

Thus Hoar is called an old woman by literary men. It is amusing to me to see the glances and smirks of men when I give Hoar his merited skirt name. I have disliked his new position so much, I would not hear him lecture even when reporting for the Press.   .   .   .   .   .   .   The Worcester papers say the County Commissioners want to borrow money to build more court-house room. We have quite too much room in the Worcester Court House for the war knaves and scoundrels of different positions. The culprits ignore the statute laws and are committing crime that will purse-feed their pockets, robbing the widow and fatherless, and snatching from them liberty, truth and justice. Once I had respect for Worcester courts—before the war. Since the war, Worcester courts would disgrace, and do, the people as a State county seat. I should no more expect a word of truth or justice from war officer courts in Worcester than I should expect to come out unburnt if dipped in a kettle of hot lead; the devil must stand aghast, being superseded by said court. The effects of our slave-war—placing in office war men, whose only qualification was to hunt, kill and rob—has so corrupted us as a nation, that iniquity rules vicegerent in Massachusetts, as they have dealt with me. Truth is squelched in said Massachusetts more than in any other State in the Union, I think. "The Jesse Pomeroy State," as I heard it called at the Centennial.

. . . . . Oh, the number of men and women who are brought up to no useful trade or calling is on the increase. Thousands of them, with their untrained powers and ignorance, find shelter in some *nook hospital*, where they may at *last draw pay*, and thus continue to exist. Morally they are pampered tramps. Worcester has the greatest supply.

E. R. HILL.

THOUGHTS.

Feb. 10.

Giants' minds are fitted by every circumstance of growth, training and habit. Great men's strength and influence are in the thoughts they suggest, not in conclusions they demonstrate. Demonstration means nothing to be done; the demonstrator carries you with him like a prisoner. Speculation is always suggestive; the speculator sends you abroad alone. Some minds are powerful generalizers; their views and reasonings are for us to conclude, if we will, whether right or wrong. Other minds are leeches, robbers, stealing the thoughts of the giants' minds.

ELIZABETH R. HILL.

WORCESTER HOSPITAL, Feb. 12th, 1878.

MRS. HASTON:—I was brought into this place, in less than two hours after you left me (in jail, 16th). My agony and terror were enough to have ended the life of ninety-nine human beings out of one hundred.

I begged them to give me a room where I might not hear the talk or see the insane. But oh! my terrible doom! My bed a hard excelsior and pillow the same, with four heavy, sickening smelling gray blankets. No bedstead, no chair, nor glass. The place to sit down was a bench recess in the iron-barred window. The heat of the room was terrible. My hope of deliverance from this terrible stone prison was gone. The heat radiators brought the most loathsome, profane, incoherent yells and shrieks around that could be made by the most raven lost minds. Before going to bed, two feeble-minded servants took me to a bath-tub, stripped me, looked me over (and its my opinion they never viewed a more perfect cleanly sweet *carcass*) with evident satisfaction at their good subject to help support this most damnable of places. And I believe in the sincerity of my heart there is not a more unknown, devilish cavern where people are placed to be got rid of. And nobody but weak unfit for anything doctors paid by State, etc., full well knowing their unfitness to earn a living but by this popular aid way. I was answered back and treated as if insane. Oh! how terrible to bear. In the night, the night watch and two night-gown attendants came in to my room to look at me. I screeched with terror, for I thought them lunatics. I stayed in that bed two nights. There had a maniac died on it Saturday before my clothes were scented with a sickening stench. I have been told it was the rubber sheet. I begged for a cooler room. Friday I had the one I have occupied since. I have a three-drawer chest, wash-stand, bowl, and pitcher, and low rocking-chair. A patient died also in this room not one week before. Drs. Eastman and Quimby came in, and told me as I had been sent there as insane, they had got to treat me as such. This was Friday, and I remonstrated. They told me explanation was useless when you are here. Oh, I see clearly they too were Dr. Tyler's confederates. Oh, to eat the same food, so poor ! to drink the same drink ; walk the same path ; live under the same banner of the insane, indeed, and have a clear understanding of all your powers, is enough to make me cry in agony hourly: My God ! why hast Thou forsaken me ?

The attendant of this bell is more of a lunatic than half of the gossiping, broken-minded women who, in their best estate, had but few half talents. She speaks and uses the most ungovernable temper toward the patients, and is abusive. I have given her my mind in her abuse to others, and she hates me with the most deadly hatred. The inmates took much interest in me, and said what are you here for—you don't look sick ; but Miss —— says I shall not talk to them. She will not allow me to repeat a verse or anything ; they all hate her, but with insane, servile fear, obey her. I never saw the person I felt ought to be horsewhipped daily more than ——. A doctor passes through usually twice a day, and speaks to the most of them. They well know they are locking and keeping a sane woman in captivity—for purpose! Oh, it is hard to put up with this insulting way they speak to me, I think, purposely to agitate me! But they find me a trump for them. My story will outvie any convent story ever read by myself, when I can get chance to tell this tale of terror, neglect, false pretence of care of those inmates who are in need of skillful physicians.

WORCESTER HOSPITAL, Feb. 12, 1878.

TRUSTEES AND SUPERINTENDENT WORCESTER HOSPITAL :

Gentlemen—I again appeal to you to direct and cause Mrs. E. R. Hill to be released from this false imprisonment. My time is money, and my money and my time have no need nor benefit from this institute which malicious designs of wicked men have hurled me into. My vigorous constitution has baffled with this unhealthy, soul-demoralizing of all places on earth to a sensitive, refined, cultivated mind. Four weeks ! long, indeed, and quite too long for reasonable investigation, as it seems to me. I cannot believe that the statute laws will permit one to be thus imprisoned who has, in every place, and situation, and calling, proven myself capable of taking care, directing wisely, discreetly, and with great frugality, all affairs. And if I can be kept longer imprisoned here, when all the above can be proven by my associates, the reason why I am kept is evident, and too infamous for comment. If Massachusetts laws will permit her Worcester county seat thus maliciously to malpractice her statute laws, to suppress truth, that the criminal proceedings of

some of North Brookfield, Mass., citizens may not be investigated.

Here I am stopped, as the trustees are just passing my stall.
I hand this part-written letter to ex-Gov. Lincoln, with a letter
written to Mr. Daniel Whiting, of North Brookfield, my neighbor, who lives about forty rods from my residence there. Gov.
Lincoln forwards them, and Mr. Whiting soon called, bringing
me some oranges his wife and sisters had sent to me. And for
that act of kindness—Mr. D. Whiting's own words to me since :
that he had had great persecution from citizens of North Brookfield for that humane act.

Gov. Lincoln was greatly perplexed and distressed at my unjust and false imprisonment, in this terrible place, for a sane,
sensitive, educated woman ! And he did his utmost to get my
release, and may the God of Truth give those men rich reward
yet ! is the prayer of that captive.

E. R. HILL.

WORCESTER HOSPITAL, Feb. 20, 1878.

MESSRS. TRUSTEES AND SUPERINTENDENT :

Gentlemen—Not expecting any more notice to-morrow than
last week from your Honorable Body, and as time is vibrating
into eternity, and I remain still in this your lunatic asylum—a
self-evident fact—for the one purpose, to ruin me for time and
eternity. I am, gentlemen, too well versed in the condition that
we, as a nation, have sunk, as it were, into general depravity.
And, sirs, I remain here in this asylum because of some ineffi-
ciency—weakness where there should be strength. There is
neither law nor justice, nor moral sentiment, nor an endeavor to
change this my unfavorable condition. Thus I have and am
kept in this heated, nervous, struggling state, since Jan. 7, 1878;
a financial benefit to this asylum since Jan. 16, 1878. My only
society is persons who come into life not only in disproportion,
not only unbalanced and unsymmetrical, but positively diseased
and in depraved condition. I was placed here by men who live
on the keen edge of ambition, and who are addicted to excesses
and violations of the statutes of God and man. And as Haman
made gallows to hang Mordecai, even so were said men likely to
end had it not been for the Masonic strength now in Worcester

courts. Their only recourse this last resort, sending E. R. Hill to your lunatic custody.

Thus you are crutching said violators of the law from statute punishment! I cannot help thinking, gentlemen, what chance is there for reformation in regard to mistakes, if they are not known, or made known, to convicts? I think it the duty of a teacher, captain, etc., to inform convicts on what line they sin, that they might work out rectification and satisfy the fractured law. If the convict is susceptible to elevation and rectification, the design of the Creator is to make a unit of him by changing the social, civil, and moral condition of said individual, not leave them to follow on in their trail of vice and delusion, through the ignorance and misconception and superstition of men. Every man who marks out a better channel of thought for his charge, every teacher who knows how to instruct men in better conditions of life, are organizing better conditions of manhood.

And, gentlemen, permit me to say here that Gabriel H. De Bevoise has been the great cause of my imprisonment in jail and transfer here; to aid the illegal proceedings of some of his parishioners, from investigation. And, sirs, the institution of organized religion, the Church, has caused more bitterness, denunciations, strifes, contentions, and persecutions, and shackles, and all kinds of oppression than any other organized institution on the globe. Had it not been for some fathers and mothers, and humble, obscure, out-of-the-way Christians in the world, such priests as said Gabriel would have carried the world to the devil long ago. Oh, could you know the full facts of the devilish proceedings of said Gabriel in plotting, ruling this imprisonment of me, E. R. Hill. And, gentlemen, is there not enough of the supernal power of God in your souls to save me from further persecution of said Gabriel and his confederates?

There is poetry and sublimity in the sentences: "He spake, and it was done." "He commanded, and it stood fast." That being the Divine method, it is, sirs, your prerogative and power to give me my liberty and my home which favors excellence, intelligence, virtue, beauty, all things divine, to-day, at this meeting of your Hon. Body.

Most respectfully,

ELIZABETH R. HILL.

Feb. 22, 1878.

My late brother William Tyler would be 55 years old, if on earth. God grant that his purified spirit in the kingdom of heaven may descend with his God and rest upon me, his sister Elizabeth, in this prison at this time of sacred invocation and commemoration of that loved brother's anniversary, together with our country's benefactor, George Washington! And as that noble brother, if on earth, would come and set me at liberty, give me back to my own well-deserved heritage, even so, O God, wilt thou not send a messenger quickly in his place to save said Elizabeth from a persecuted death?

Were not the first principles laid down by our Revolutionary fathers, the nobility of men? Whatever degrades him—whatever corrupts and injures his moral, intellectual, and physical well-being, is inimical to the well-being of society, to the State, to the whole country. Has not this country become so absorbed in schemes for amassing wealth and power, that their eyes are closed to the moral aspects of society? This moral apathy has allowed systems to grow and expand until they are fast becoming controlling elements in the government. There are elements in our society which are fatal to all true progress and true liberty, thus becoming instruments of barbarism. Who could have prophesied that, in Republican America, such atrocities would be protected by the strong arm of the law, thus warming the serpents into power for evil. Can truth and all we hold sacred here be trampled under foot by certain societies to serve party purposes, thus making a plague spot in our government? Oh, men in power, be not deceived longer; take the first step in reform, and restore all pure moral and intellectual humanity to social and true liberty, and then protect them even if necessary as our fathers protected Bunker Hill a century ago, is the prayer of the captive.

ELIZABETH R. HILL.

Feb. 23.

Mr. J. Gilman and Abbot called this afternoon. The face of some friends in this prison is a comfort; but, O God, direct them or some person to take off the chain with which evil men have shackled me in this prison almost six weeks without reason but their own misdoings. I am daily convinced of the terrible power of money to suppress truth and cover crime. That and that alone stays me in this maniac prison. The man who possesses wealth possesses power, but it is power to do evil as well as good.

———

The beauties of this lovely morning are the result of Divine skill. They are complete in themselves ; to be enjoyed, the mind must be in harmony with them. Obedience acts upon the mind like an inspiration, and God grant this, Thy holy day, that deeds of charity, kindness, justice to all may be renewed in the hearts of men, thus giving power and wisdom to men to assist the widow and fatherless, to open the prison door to the upright and pure in heart and life.

> " Mankind is slow, but God is swift,
>   And they who give Him oar
> On Truth's blue billows are adrift,
>   Ere others launch from shore.
> Ho, brethren on the crystal tide,
>   At no far distant time,
> The masses shall be at your side,
>   In sympathy sublime !"

E. R. HILL.

———

My spirit is shrouded in gloom this morning, crushing my life out like a worm at the root.

O God ! open the eyes and understanding of my friends that they may hasten to me with honest and manly spirits, determined to release me from this maniac prison. Hasten, O God, the fresh hour of relief, when my fellow-men will grapple this wicked persecution, and with legal force, with one mighty effort, release me from all persecution and malice of the North Brookfield railroad and De Bevoise mob, and restore me to my cottage home and its blessings, thus making my heart leap with joy.

ELIZABETH R. HILL.

WORCESTER HOSPITAL, Feb. 27, 1878.

Messrs. TRUSTEES, SUPERINTENDENT, AND DOCTORS:

Gentlemen—Six weeks to-day since I have been in this Insane prison. Gentlemen, this bright, spring-like morning, when nature beams in sunlight beauty, and you and your household are enjoying the out-door exercise, can you not bestow a God-like duty upon a lady who has appealed to you in divers ways to give me a helping hand at this time of legal persecution emergency? Gentlemen, you will do me great discredit to even think that I (E. R. Hill) would disabuse any assistance you might give me in discharging me from this retreat. And whatever your advice might or may be to me in regard to unjustness of the court proceedings, in their transactions of the several cases pending of which you have been informed, and my book explains, I would most gladly receive any direction as kindly as any sister, wife, or daughter, whose every desire is for peace, purity, and godliness.

And, sirs, are not the best principles of man made manifest in their interest to help others, to give them a start, to relieve their shackles, to get them above-board? Oh, sirs, do not leave me longer to struggle and tug under this burden, which I cannot throw off without your special assistance!

To me gentlemen there is something mysterious why I am not permitted the right of statute and human investigation, and I have appealed to you as men of honor to see and investigate into my several persecutions set forth in my book, to do as those stubborn facts demand, if you were in my place. Would you have your property taken to make others rich, illegally? Would you be taken from your own property without warrant or cause, and put into a lock-up and let out like a beast, black-mailed to destroy your character? Would you be deprived of the right of getting your living honorably, laboriously, and with guarded, wise frugality? Would you have your property burned by incendiaries and then be deprived of the privilege of finding out who the firebug was, if possible? Would you think it right to have a walnut-tree nuisance, that is, the picking, clubbing, throwing stones upon a walnut tree, to fall upon your loved, lost, beautiful children's grave, thus desecrating the most sacred of all places on earth? Would you like to be imprisoned because you tried within the pale of statute law to remove said nuisance from your holy of holiest consecrated grave plot and lot ? Would you like to have the men who imprisoned you illegally, perhaps, bail you out without your consent, and dispose of you by chicanery, placing you in a lunatic retreat ?

Would you like to be deprived of your home by those who have never guided, directed, nor helped you in any way to get together your property, or even visited you, nor cared for you, even when you sought them; and they gave no heed—not so much as a bow was given—then have them put you away from your sacred home comforts, to cover the above-mentioned question from investigation.

Dr. Eastman questioned me in regard to the price of my book, issued Dec. 29, 1877. Gentlemen, I made a careful contract, fulfilled it, and enlarged said contract and fulfilled the same. And, gentlemen, I can prove by all concerned my capability for business, as being shrewd, wise, most careful of expense to be avoided, ever planning my purposes beforehand, weighing them with great caution, as I alone must lose or gain financially by my literary attempts, which my circumstances and persecution have caused me to set forth, instead of recourse to the courts, where I as a woman am despised because of my truth and uprightness—has not the least possible chance to vindicate herself against money, and which rules with powerful sway to cover crime. And, gentlemen, I ask for nothing but truth as it is before Almighty God, and I can bring proof to your Honorable Body by friends who know me, at home and abroad—that is, across that river that empties into the Atlantic.

But oh, gentlemen, let no time be lost in vain attempts for subterfuge to cover the sins of those men; but know, fully and distinctly, that have I no hope for remuneration than what I might gain by a Worcester tedious court, myself to pay the necessary bills and then have what might be decreed by petty jury. I should say let me have what I know I have in peace and quiet in my own little home, which needs me to-day using my ability to restore that building they have destroyed ! and even they accused me, report has it, it was my work !

Gentlemen, I do implore you to demand of Luther Deland that he answer to that charge of crime, report has it, he has blackmailed me—E. R. Hill. Gentlemen, that accounts for telegrams not being answered. You must see how little said Luther has done for me in cases before this last insurance blackmail. That he has held the office of deputy-sheriff too long is self-evident to one who is acquainted with the blood, that a little extra advancement in position acts detrimental to their mental organization. His mother, uncle, and aunts have died insane. Therefore, with charity I shall deal with said person, for I have evidence of his weakening faculties manifested by his injudicious acts and sayings. And I further declare I have meant and did wish the investigation of the appealed case of Sept. 14, 1878.

The doings of the court are convincing to me they were not willing me to have statute investigation. The De Bevoise case I wish settled, not by a farce court like the 14th of September, but one, first and last, in the Superior Court; which has been denied me. And, gentlemen, I have no money to be taken by their illegal manipulations of the law. I do not need any advice on the railroad case; that is in safe deposit. And, sirs, my absence from my home is a financial loss to me. My work needs doing now before spring work begins, and as I can prove by my past life, there is no one more capable of managing, restoring, and bringing round crooked, disarranged affairs, and almost making the " desert waste bud and blossom like the rose."

Dr. Tyler has not been a guide nor adviser, but he is my brother, whom I could forgive and never dig up the wound, but I could never desire him as an adviser, never, no never; but could ever treat him as though the past were not, so far as cherishing ill-feelings is concerned. I cannot talk about my affairs with those who would wrong the widow and orphan ! My every desire is for truth and honor, and I have never, no never compounded nor practised hypocrisy in its various phases ; but, with high spirit, turned from all wrong-doing in public, private, or whatever situation I have, by the mysterious Providence of God, been called to pass through. I do not ignore my right to be released from my unjust, inhuman burdens or shackles the wicked have or may bind me with, and I beg you to break the shackles, open the prison-door, and tell E. R. Hill to go to her home.

E. R. HILL.

WORCESTER HOSPITAL, March 2, 1878.

My father, David Tyler, North Brookfield, was borne to the silent tomb fourteen years ago to-day. The services were attended by the Rev. St. John, Universalist minister of this city. That beautiful, placid countenance of my loved father in that rosewood casket, so still in death, I see as clear as if before me this day ; and God grant that sanctified, father spirit may come from the throne of God and rest upon his daughter, Elizabeth in this maniac prison. Oh, give her of Thy holy spirit wisdom and power as it is and has been given to those in bonds through the sedition of men, and to make this rod of affliction hedged in by thorns given by man to me as a scourge be made a weapon of strength, through the infinite love of my father and my father's God ! May it bring reform to our courts, and cause an overthrow of all in authority of statute laws who do not abide by its precepts, as they are set forth to be in harmony with the Divine commands.

E. R. HILL.

Above sketch of my father's death, written just before going out to breakfast the last time with those weak, incoherent, mental lost women. " Oh, God, come quick, I pray, and release me. Come, God of truth, come !" Thus I constantly prayed there. About 10 A.M., William Gile, attorney-at-law (to whom I sent a letter the day previous), came to my captive abode and called to see me, &c. The servant on the ward in which I was held captive came to me and asked how I sent this letter to Esquire Gile ? I told her to tell the M.D.'s, God sent me a messenger, and more to say to the same men that you were not instrumental in sending for said Gile, Esq., and for further information they would have to wait till they get home to God. Esquire Gile inquired and found I had not manifested insanity, &c., and came into my room and told me Judge Chapin wished me released, and said Judge opposed bitterly my being sent to said Asylum without court of some of my neighbors; but was overruled, as it seems, by the Railroad DeBevoise mob. Esquire Gile then proceeded to get papers from Probate Court for my release, and said Gile had me taken from said captivity about 4:30 P. M. of March 2, 1878, anniversary of my father's burial.

Said Gile accompanied me home to North Brookfield, stopping at my neighbor (at my request), Mr. Haston, the same house and friends I was carried to by the perjurer Bothwell, January 5, and taken from January 7 to jail. Mr. and Mrs. Haston were just sitting down to tea table as Esquire Gile and I entered that home. Oh reader, imagine for a moment that meeting. I had written three as good letters to be sent them from that maniac ark as ever I wrote in my life. Said Haston never received one of them, but with great anxiety would inquire of my situation, and Warren Tyler and bonum Nye would speak of me as hopelessly insane. Think, reader, of that blasphemous, blackmailing, lying of those men. And, reader, not two hours before Esquire Gile and Elizabeth R. Hill entered that attractive, beautiful home of said Haston, who had just come from little bonum magnum Nye, to know how I was; and, reader, that bonum magnum Nye told Mr. Haston: "Mrs. Hill is very wild; it will be a long time before she will be here again, if ever." And Mr. Haston had but just rehearsed that damnable of all lies of Nye's to his wife about E. R. Hill. Mr. and Mrs. Haston were as surprised to see me enter as if one had descended from above, they said. I ask candidly, reader, if the lie Ananias and Sapphira told, which, according to Scripture, God caused them to fall dead, where will Nye—Tyler yet get swift retribution? I was as much a lunatic then as ever I had been, and the person is not on earth under heaven among men, that could say I ever was, and speak the truth. And that Railroad DeBevoise Mob maliciously placed me there to keep me from bringing them to legal tribunal. Of course, at Mr. Haston's, we were full of talk, Mr. and Mrs. Pope and family were all glad to see me home again. The above letters written in captivity and the letters I wrote for patients getting them out to their homes, and the many scenes of horror I had witnessed held them unweary listeners.

Next morning was Sabbath, March 3. After breakfast I went to Walnut Grove Cemetery, where my four loved-lost beautiful boys lie in the grave so low; and to my father's, mother's, Brothers William's, Albert's, and Charlotte's graves—passing my cottage home and the house of my birth. On returning I went into my house (which had been vacant since September 27), the barn burned, my yard strewed with burnt timbers, and boxes of goods part burned strewed in every direction. Nothing except what one wanted had been picked up—the rest looked an incendiary field—the very results of the Railroad DeBevoise Mob. I was up in my parlor looking at my dead boy's picture, in the very room where the funeral service of three of my beautiful boys had been held. I heard man's steps, I went to the basement, and there stood Warren Tyler, M.D., who had aided my imprisonment. His face, every muscle twitching with fiendish anger, and same kind of voice says: "How come you home here?" I replied I came here because it's my home, and my right to be here from which I have been kept by conspirators. He advances, as if to clutch me, saying: "Tell me how you got here?" I said I guess if it is Sunday you can find out what lawyer has obtained my release from that fearful hell, which you and others had falsely imprisoned me in. Warren wilted; in another moment with clenched fist upraised, he says: " You report false imprisonment, and I hear of it, I will have you back again in less than forty-eight hours." I stood my ground well; but oh, I ought to have been a man then, just a few minutes. No more.

Monday, 4th inst., Warren Tyler and Gabriel DeBevoise are riding together past the window I am sitting at. They are in perplexed, deep, anxious conversation, as if, plain written, what shall we do? And all those who caused this malicious imprisonment of me (E. R. Hill) were asking: " How did she get out?" "I should like to know how she got out. How did she get out?" And more crest fallen two legged species of manhood never was seen according to report than that Railroad DeBevoise mob were. And at the great merriment of my friends, which I must say, some were a little weak in the backbone to say what they thought. And as for me, I felt the waters of Jordan, Abannar, and Parphar could not wash and soak out the stench I had inhaled into my system, and give me back my vigorous strength which had been reduced by being kept from out-door exercise and from the sun, and in that terrible poisoning air to me. Everything in that maniac ark is calculated to destroy a well, noble, pure-minded person. Thus I was crushed, and in God's time and way, with the wisdom He should give me, I set about soaking, purging myself of what had been inoculated into me in that maniac hell, from which to which I can never think but with disgust and horror. And I pray Almighty God to bring upon every one their every word and act with which those malignant men falsely imprisoned me there. And if there is a God of justice and truth, it will come upon them.

Tuesday, 5th.—I went over to my cottage home, built fires in the stoves to dry and also to ventilate my house—Mrs. Haston assisting me to get ready to go to New York. I left there about 4 P.M., and went to Mr. Charles Kittridge, where Bothwell arrested me. And oh, how good it is to meet friends! I stayed over night. Next morning Mrs. Kittridges, with carriage, conveyed me to East Brookfield depot. There I buy ticket for that Worcester city, to insurance man, to get my moiety of insurance. It is paid, and I remove my insurance to another Company. I then pay Esq. Gile, for getting me out of that captivity, which cost me to get out, $49.50. I then went to Savings Bank in Mechanic Hall Building, and withdrew from said bank my deposit of $450, losing my interest on the same since January. I then proceed on to that Courthouse where all the chicanery had been consummated, and made copy of Grand Jury indictment, and of the application of Co. Commissioners, heretofore printed, and was at the Great Union depot, Worcester, at 7 P.M. of said 6th inst., with my ticket bought for New York Steamboat train, arriving in New York next day—7th inst.—about 6 A.M. I proceeded at once where my collaterals were held, and paid my bill, and also went to my dear friend, who seems so like Mrs. Beecher, who died in 1870, and paid her $10, due. I called on several friends; each and every one rejoiced to see me, and hear my late facts of my terrible captivity, returning home on the 4.30 steamboat train to Worcester, thence on the street to Esq. Gile's office ; I found the train had gone which I meant to meet, and returned to my home at once. Esq. Gile said I could go up on 10 o'clock express. I told him that train did not stop at East Brookfield; he persisted it did. I told him Bates had had it changed then since my captivity, but Gile was mistaken, and my conveyance landed me at West Brookfield. I called at Mr. Adolphus Hampleton's, whose sons and daughters had been under my instruction many terms, and people of high, noble repute. How much soul there was in our greeting! . . . They were greatly surprised to think, amid all my persecutions in that fearful captivity, I could write such letters as I read

them. . . . And I will interpolate here the letter of
Feb. 20, I read to Dr. Quimby. He told me after reading it, that
some twenty to thirty senators, representatives, and doctors
were going to pass through this hall in about one hour. (This
hall was between two wards.) M.D. says, " Stay here, and ask
them to hear your petition for release." Accordingly, when the
room was full, I rose from my seat, and said, " Gentlemen, will
you please hear this letter read I hold in my hand, which I wrote
yesterday." Those who had not seen me there were surprised—if
face-expression ever speaks truth—at my presence there, as any
candid person might know. After reading, Dr. Hooper says,
" We must see Gabriel at once." With tone, I hope, will be
visited upon his own head, in God's time—a half talented M.D.,
not much to answer for to be sure; and a Col. Washburn, who
has name of one wing of that maniac hell—he is also made of
money, not brains—he did not notice the reading. Others
were anxious to know the whole story. And report has it, that
letter caused a law to be passed that session in the Boston Legislature, that no person should be imprisoned to suppress
or stop lawsuits hereafter, etc. The Superintendent of provisions
for that maniac ark was Daniel W. Bemis, a scholar of mine in
1842. He said to some senator, as they passed me, " This is,
or was, my teacher when a boy." I replied, " And as much insane then as now." He says, " It will not be very long before
you will get out, *Court stops soon.*" The first time I saw D. W.
B. after my captivity, he told me to keep up good spirits, I
should not be there long. I said, " I wish to go to-morrow before the Grand Jury." Bemis says, " Those men who put you
here wo'nt let you." I asked him if Worcester courts had become thus corrupt, that this most fearful of all inquisitions
should be given me, because I wished to have the *crimes, theft,
blackmail, incendiarism investigated,* as statutes provide? Bemis
says, "Mrs. Hill, if I was in your place, as quick as you get out
I would sell my property in North Brookfield, and find a home
where I could live in peace." I said, " That I shall not do.
On that principle every thief, highwayman, incendiary, ought to
be allowed free access wherever their devilish purposes lead
them. And no highwayman or assassin is guilty of a greater
crime than those who have caused my incarceration here. My
home and that of my fathers, is sacred to me, and no place could

I live alone but where my loved children were born, sickened, and died. Every spot and place is sacred in memory's hall. My children seem about me at home. Oh, my sacred, quiet, loved home! how I long for thee!"

Mr. Bemis I used to see once a week generally, and he always said, "Keep up good courage, you will be out soon." Oh! but Bemis little knew the terrible plot of those two-legged species of manhood Every one of them would have gladly kept me there till I died, with as much exultation as any savage ever scalped a white victim. And those men's chagrin at not ending my life, and thus keep me from telling this inquisition of the nineteenth century, which will be as much history a few years hence as Massachusetts Salem witchcraft.

Reader, it is worthy of consideration whether persecution by torture, imprisonment, or any kind of inquisition ever was beneficial to the morals of society? And, readers, I have never, throughout my past life done any act, thought, or word, which should deprive me of my liberty or my rights. I have always been law abiding, and I have endeavored always to speak the truth, and the truth only. And my statements upon these pages are correct, and I only exercise the rights of an American citizen, which the North Brookfield Railroad DeBevoise persecutors have, and are depriving me of. And every libel attached to my name has been done on the same principle that John Hancock was arrested in Boston, on a "misdemeanor" in 1768.

King George III. spoke in his Parliament of the patriots of Boston as "those turbulent and seditious persons." It was moved in Parliament to address the king " to bring to condign punishment " such men as Otis, Adams, and Hancock. Chief Justice Hutchinson declared Samuel Adams " the greatest incendiary in the king's dominions." True, Samuel Adams lit a fire which burned not only in Boston, but throughout New England and all the American colonies, until freedom reigned. And is that freedom to be trampled under foot by illegal railroad corporations, in the last quarter of the nineteenth century? Samuel Adams declared "Acts of Parliament against natural equity are void." Almighty God! raise up men to declare the decisions of the modern courts, which are against natural equity, void.

I will here inform my readers of the two faces W. Tyler, M. D., wore in this my persecution. When the mob had E. R. H. in the lock-up, W. T. was asked why he did not get me out at once ? Tyler said it would make trouble with his wife. Again, when E. R. H. was on the railroad train for Worcester jail, Warren Tyler told conductor Bryant these words: "Mrs. Hill has always taken care of herself without help, and she will now." Other said at times, W. T. would talk as if he were my brother and again as an enemy. Many men and women have told me when it was reported that the mob had made a transfer to the lunatic abode, Warren T was questioned why ? W. T. said "E. R. H. is not crazy at all, but we have sent her to that asy-lum to put an end to my having law suits." Others would in-terrogate my imprisonment. W. T. would speak sympatheti-cally for me, and aver I was treated thus because I told Bates and his posse too many truths, and they would not stand it. And thus W. T. made those people believe he was not the cause in any way of my imprisonment. And, readers, since it has actually offended those people when I told them W. T. and Gabriel did more then any others in the work. After said con-spirators had me in the insane hell, Warren Tyler set about to *get a guardian* over E. H. R. But the *perjurer could not get one*, but was told E. R. H. was more capable than they of taking care of my property.

And report has it that W. T. had to pay all costs of that plot, etc., out of his own pocket. Yes, and it would be justice if his every dollar were filched from him and others, as they have conspired to take from me and mine.

I will say I wrote a letter to my son, L. K. Hill, Centreville, Wayne Co., Ind., on the third day I was in that terrible maniac hell and read it to Dr. Eastman, Superintendent, asking him if he would mail it to my son. The doctor told me he would, and that letter was never received by my son. I had written true statements of my terrible imprisonment by Warren Tyler and others. Tears dropped from Eastman's eyes as I read the fear-ful tale. I also found on coming to New York, that the letters I wrote and gave to Superintendent Marble, of schools in Wor-cester city, to mail, were never received. On my return from New York, January 8, 1878, I called on Marble and Davis, and asked where those letters were I gave them in my captivity to send to parties in New York. Oh ! how crestfallen thus to be brought to conviction. I demanded my letters. They gave them up. I then told Davis it was a pity he could not see the broom put over his own daughters' back in her mental lost condition. And, sir, I have stood many times between her and the upraised broom. When I gave you and Marble the letters I did not know that the Davis girl was your daughter; neither did I know that at that very time Superintendent Marble was "putting away his wife." Had I known those facts you men would not have had those letters. And you further have proved your readiness to aid the mob. Marble I always had respected when meeting him at teachers' institutes. I now pity his put-away wife.

WEST UPTON, AUGUST 30, 1875.

ELIZABETH R. HILL:

In looking over my letters this morning, I found yours of August 6, unopened. It must have been received in my absence and overlooked. This is my apology for not answering your note at once.

Before the Commissioners can act in your case a petition must be presented to them in open session, describing the land taken, and on that a motion must be legally served on the Railroad corporation, a time appointed for the hearing, and so forth. We shall be in session next Friday, October 3, in Worcester, when you can present your petition.

With respect, VELORIOUS TAFT.

WEST UPTON, SEPTEMBER, 11, 1875.

ELIZABETH R. HILL:

Yours of the 11th inst. is at hand. We made the appointment at the Town Hall, because it is a public place and we must meet somewhere. We shall open the court there, take a view of the land in question and then the further hearing can be heard at your house or any other proper place that you may suggest. There will be no need of you being at the Town house, as all that will be done there will be an opening of the court and an adjurnment to the land taken.

With respect, VELORIOUS TAFT,
Chairman of Commissioners.

NORTH BROOKFIELD, SEPTEMBER 9, 1875.

MESSRS. BACON, HOPKINS AND BACON:

Gentlemen, Cannot the hearing be at my residence? I have a reception room 16½ feet square, and am on the main road from North to East Brookfield, two-thirds of the distance from the Town Hall to my land.

I did not think of the notoriety which must attend my going to the Hall etc., which is appalling to me.

I supposed the commissioners come quietly and appraise the property without prejudice, "as informed." Are those directors and the Town people all to be present at the hearing? If so I wish to be early informed. My residence is far the most suitable place for the hearing, and I pray that there the interview will be. The commissioners meet October 14, on the roads, etc. Is my hearing to be the 15th of this month, or next?

The contractor told me yesterday, the Railroad on my land will be all completed ready for sleepers etc., this week.

I have not spoken to any one that I am to have an hearing, and shall not unless legally ordered.

Respectfully,   E. R. HILL.

_____

AUGUST 6TH.

On the third day of October, A.D. 1875, Elizabeth R. Hill filed her petition before the Honorable County Commissioners of the said county, praying them to assess your petitioner's damages in the premises, and to order all such culverts, cattle guards, and crossings and obstructions as were necessary and proper to be made by said Railroad Company, and that they give security for your petitioner's damages and costs. And a hearing was had thereafter on said petition on the 15th day of October, A.D. 1875, after due notice to all the parties; and the said Commissioners, on the first day of December, 1875, completed and returned their award in the Clerk's office of said county, awarding your petitioner a sum of money in damages which your petitioner considers insufficient compensation for her damage; and the said Commissioners also ordered that said corporation should construct a grade crossing at grade across said railroad, near the south end of the second tract aforesaid, for the purpose of enabling the said Hill, her heirs and assigns, to transfer their crops growing on said lands, the same to be properly planked on both sides of said crossing, which is forever to be maintained by said company, and bars to be erected or gates each side of said crossing, and said bars or gates to be forever maintained by said company, all of which is in addition to said sum of money so awarded.

And your petitioner says she is aggrieved by the doings of the Commissioners in the premises, and asks that she may have trial by a jury at the bar of your honorable court, and that your petitioner's damage may be assessed by said jury, and that she may have such other relief as the case requires.

ELIZABETH R. HILL,
By P. C. Bacon, her Att'y.

Worcester, Nov. 29th, 1876.

COMMONWEALTH OF MASSACHUSETTS, }
Worcester, s. s. : }

Office of the Clerks of the Superior Court at Worcester.
In Vacation, November 29th, A.D. 1876.

On the petition aforesaid it is ordered, That the petitioner notify the said North Brookfield Railroad Company to appear at the Term of this Court, to be holden at Worcester aforesaid, on the first Monday of March next, by serving said company with an attested copy of said petition and this order, thirty days at least before the sittings of said court, that said company may then and there show cause why the prayer of said petition should not be granted.

Attest:
JOSEPH NASON, *Clerk*.

1955.

E. R. HILL,
Petition,

vs.

NORTH BROOKFIELD R. R. CO.,
For a Jury Trial
Before Sup. Court.
Filed, Nov. 29th, 1876.
Attest:
J. MASON, *Clerk*.

BACON, HOPKINS, BACON.

No. BROOKFIELD, May 6th, 1876.

North Brookfield R. R. Directors—Addressed:

SIRS—I herewith enter complaint to you, that the fence upon both sides of the entire length of the North Brookfield R. R., cutting my two mowings into right and obtuse angles (the profile of which you have upon the North Brookfield R. R. chart), removing heavy stone wall, despoiling the location, and ruining my income from said mowings, and rendering them unsafe for the protection of cattle, or the entrance of the same, or building thereon. Also obstructing the drive way between my walnut-grove and lower mowing, "which the County Commissioners have directed you to grade," the copy of the same you have. I remonstrated with you, directors and selectmen, before you encroached and severed my land, against such a proceeding. You gave no heed to my legal warning. In open defiance to my appeal and the statutes, you took possession, removed, obstructed, and debarred me—*yes, robbed me* of my own legal rights. And, Sirs, you will take heed to my complaint, that you must comply with the Revised Statutes of 1874, page 220 to 225. And if you neglect to comply with the provisions there named, you will be subjected to the fine named in sect. 84, page 224 and 225. And you must not permit *Freeman Walker,* a *deadly enemy to me,* to act as committee, or negotiate in any way conceivable in this my R. R. proceeding.

I remain,

ELIZABETH R. HILL.

———

NORTH BROOKFIELD, Aug. 30th, 1877.

To the Treasurer of North Brookfield:

I hereby give notice that I pay the tax assessed upon me for this year under protest, and consider the same unjust and illegal.

E. R. HILL.

SUPERIOR COURT.

WORCESTER, *s. s.:*   Dec. 5th, 1877.

ELIZ. R. HILL, Pet.,
vs.
NORTH BROOKFIELD R. R. Co.

We petitioner moves their case be placed at the foot of the
trial list of this term—to take place at the March term trial list—
with this understanding, that it is not to be tried at this term.

> **ELIZ. R. HILL,**
> By her Att'y,
>
> W. II. B. HOPKINS,
> SPECIALLY.

———

I will ask my readers to think of me clearing up the ruins of
that incendiary fire, and not one effort on the part of the town,
only the "form printed and posted, offering $500 reward for the
detection of the incendiary." No notice was taken of the parties who ought to have been, and whom I desired to have the
Insurance Co. investigate ; and I have had this loss. No remuneration or aid, but this small pittance of insurance. But those
who caused that fire may an Omniscient God bring to justice.
And, oh, to find my large, deep box, containing my autobiogra-
phy and other important documents and memorials, gone from
my *sacred* room. And scores of other valuables filched from my
house, was hard to bear. I often say it seems a great wrong that
all fire bugs, thieves, libelers, assassins, highwaymen, perjurers,
liars, cannot be struck right off, like Lot's wife, and many others. It's my opinion the earth then would soon get moralized.

But to be on my own land in my own house was happiness
(notwithstanding the terrible pollution). As fast as my strength
would permit, I tried to make repairs. I sickened, but few ad-
ministered aid. One's friends and foes in such times of need are
plainly seen. My enemies on the part of women, which are representatives of households, are those who through envy of my
straightforward, educative, truthful abilities, renders me unpop-
ular in their eyes, &c. Reader, I am obliged to say the above,
for it is truth. And I say it as the afflicted Job in the Scripture
replied to Bildad and others, his wife not excepted.

First Monday in April after my return from captivity, I went to town meeting as reporter—the position I had held since Dec., 1874. That I was expected was evident; the very Lombard, who had so gentlemanly seated me before, stood with Southworth at the entrance of the hall, one hand on attic door (or *gallery*), speaking hurriedly: "Mrs. Hill, you must be seated up stairs." I made no reply; passed up (which act to this minute I regret), and such hatred, vindictive expression, as was on H. Knight, C. Adams, Jr., Freeman Walker, Bates, Bothwell, and some others, I shall remember till I meet them at the throne of God. The effluvia arising from tobacco, &c., soon caused me to withdraw. I often have wondered if men wrangled in other town meetings as is the case in N. Brookfield.

I did my own business as before captivity. And it was a very notable fact, those *men* who had caused my captivity and loss (with exception of two) would raise their hat in bowing, and more, which to me merited a cool return. In May I had notice of my father's sister Hannah's death, 96 years of age. I attended the funeral, for I had the greatest respect for her, as all others did who knew her. Her life was single, but virtue, integrity, activity, gave her length of days. My grandfather, Captain Moses Tyler, was one of the most noted, public spirited and influential men of his day, are the sayings of Freeman Walker who knew him. That funeral service of my aged aunt is in memory's-hall. During the summer months I sold some of my Histories, at the great chagrin of T. C. Bates; he has tried every way not to have people purchase them. In words of the late Curtis Stoddard and other notables, the facts, truths, therein stated are too much for the unscrupulous T. C. B., who is climbing the ladder of wealth by the ruin of others, though he does many very worthy acts; but to those who know him it is his self-aggrandizement, not love to mankind, that gives for no return. Bates gives to buy office, power. Ambition rules him with such sway, were the bygones of two centuries ago now, many heads would be off that now are on shoulders. But the modern Bates and contemporaries have a worse inquisition, in my opinion, which is to dispose of those who interrogate their illegal acts by placing them in a lunatic hell. It was said of T. C. Bates in 1875, when the North Brookfield R. R. was in construction, he was actually mentally upset at two different times, owing to excessive mental labor. His wife also, it was feared, would be crazy at the time of the death of her mother, who died at an *insane retreat*, and had been there confined once or twice before this last sickness. T. C. B. has a pretty daughter, born about the time of its grandmother's death. It would be quite natural result if insanity should yet be the cup T. C. Bates will yet drink to its dregs.

I will here speak again of Gabriel. One Friday evening, the first week in May after my captivity, I was standing at the grave of my babes, and Gabriel came to his lot adjoining mine. An Irishman had felled those three old walnut trees, and not one left but Gabriel's ; Isaac May, committee, had told me just before that Gabriel would not consent to have his tree cut. Says May, "It is a nuisance, and I have always said it. They all were." The expression on G. H. DeB.'s face was not, at this time at the grave of his late wife and daughter, grief, nor prayer meeting, but the comedian, comic trickster. He glibly says : "Good evening, Mrs. Hill." I looked at him, and said: "Gabriel, Committee May has just told me you will not consent to have that old walnut tree on your lot cut. You are part owner of that lot—16 feet square—which is your only real estate ; on it stands a nuisance, which is desired by others as well as myself to be cut down, for the trimming of which (by my monument man, which has been said by many, improved its looks), you, Gabriel, have caused me to be imprisoned ; your own complaint to the town and committee! The words of L. Brewer, committee, which you demanded, were, 'that they (the town) should prosecute me, or you would,' as they readily did. And you gave the job. Now, Gabriel (he stands right still), you are going to prayer meeting ; now, when you get up to exhort and direct the sheep into the fold of Christ, and tell them the dangers and temptations in their path, you tell them what temptations you have this day been able to resist. Tell them *that grave-yard committee* have been trying to make you give consent that they may cut down your walnut tree on your grave lot, but you were enabled to resist them through Christ. Oh, Gabriel, see your spirit ; would not you be very likely to let a Railroad Co. take your real estate and despoil your beautiful house lots in open disregard to the statute form of taking lands for public purposes ? You are willing my property should be taken, worth thousands, and have no equity, and you will not give up an old tree not worth $2, and the committee told you they would cut up the wood for you and deliver it to your door. Oh, how you shine in Christ's spirit! Behold your garment!!!" The Irishman heard what I said; and when G. H. De B. passed by, says the man: "Mrs. Hill, your talk to him will put the axe to that tree to-morrow." Reader, in the morning G. H. De B. told May to cut the tree down.

And that old 50 year old walnut tree was rotten, hollow, the whole length of its butt, worthless for timber or wood. I said to the wood *cutter* that inside rottenness of that tree is a perfect representation of the rotten emptiness of the religion of G. H. DeBevoise.

Gabriel was remarried the memorable month he caused me to be imprisoned. A few weeks later I was at my babies' grave (which is a brick vault in the ground, in which is a marble shelf, above those babies' coffins, to rest my coffin on when my earthly work is done), with sickle, clipping grass, to make and keep the plot clean, neat, &c., for I loved to be there, thinking their spirits lingered round the spot, and as far as I was pure in spirit I could commune with them. . . . As I sat there living in sacred memory, of a sudden Gabriel and the *new* wife came up back of me, bringing some expensive bouquets to decorate the grave of his late wife, his wife taking the large bouquet from Gabriel's hands, saying, "Let me place it." Gabriel had made an attempt to stoop, and did not. I thought he had a stitch of lumbago; neither did he walk quite natural as he goes to bring another bouquet, his wife placing it also. No notice was taken of my presence. But I volunteered thus: "Mr. De Bevoise, you come here with beautiful flowers to place over your lost one's grave, and the passers-by will say how fragrant those flowers are. And you, sir, have done your mightiest to cover my babies' graves with disgrace, fragrant as if dipped from the bowels of hell." His wife steps forward, extends her hand, and says: "Mrs. Hill, you're mistaken; my husband is your friend." I said: "Mrs. De Bevoise, I know you are not knowing to what I mean." Mrs. De B. says: "I have heard." I said: "What you may have heard and the facts of the case are two different things. Your husband has caused me to be blackmailed, imprisoned as a criminal, and his motive was selfish, and to aid the illegal railroad out, if possible, of their pit which their violations of statue had drawn them in.

"And my prayer to an omnipotent, omniscient, omnipresent God is—if he is a prayer-hearing God—to smite Gabriel II. De Bevoise with some physical calamity that will be made most public, and that I may know my prayer is answered. For God, in His mysterious providence, is making me, a lone woman, a " battle axe." Men are against me, but I know God is for me, and will yet vindicate me—for my every desire for over fifty-two years has been truth, virtue, justice, and mercy, doing all the good I could, ever doing as I would be done by ; speaking the truth at all times and in all places, and never violating statute laws of man or God. Come quick, Almighty God—come, smite Gabriel II. De Bevoise, and cause him to be removed from this my native town, which his selfish will has disgraced. Mrs. De Bevoise extended her hand again, saying : " Mrs. Hill, you are mistaken about my husband, and if you ever need help come to us." My soul recoiled, and the Scripture passage found utterance ; thus, even so the devil made offer, but was not accepted. Gabriel spoke not one word, but looked an indescribable compound.

I expect some readers will say the above is a vindictive spirit. But, reader, please remember I have been falsely imprisoned, blackmailed ; my property has been stolen, burned, and I am deprived of the rights of an American citizen. I therefore wrestle in agonizing prayer to an omnipotent God to plead my cause, and make men know, and feel, that man's extremity is God's opportunity. G. H. De Bevoise, on returning from said cemetery, as report had it, "in getting out of his business wagon, stepped out over the wheel," the horse starting at the same time, causing said Gabriel to be severely set down astride of the wheel, injuring him so badly that medical assistance was called to dress the unmentionable wound. Report had it, and newspapers also, that said Gabriel was a great sufferer, and exceedingly nervous. In two or three days said wound was lanced by Dr. W. Tyler, which discharged freely, thereby giving relief to said G., but like as a carbuncle keeps one upon a bed of suffering three or four or more months, that length of time and more was Gabriel H. De Bevoise kept with his unmentionable sickness, and it called forth many and many ludicrous remarks, and from his own church parishioners as well as others ; they loudly affirmed that, in accordance with Scripture, G. II. De Bevoise would have no scriptural right to preach in the synagogue, for he " was not without blemish." But some of his sisters in the church were heard to express " their grief at being unable to administer to him in his sickness," but they "felt and knew it was a holy sickness." When those sisters' lamentations were told me, I remarked: " I hoped said sisters would thus feel toward every other man, young or old, who might be called to thus sicken, etc." And the ladies kept his bed showered with flowers to manifest their tender sympathies, I suppose ; and never in my life was there in my native town a sickness that made the " ha! ha!"— the ludicrous remarks, and the smirks at the mention of Gabriel's (unmentionable) sufferings, which the " men said must be most terrible." Fortunate for Gabriel he was at this time in full fellowship with the great infidel W. T., M.D. (and it is my opinion Gabriel never sought to change his unbelief); but was aiding, yes, crushing out the cause of Christ by his very acts. W. T. was indefatigable in his care of suffering Gabriel—and W. T. told some of *his lady friends* how much he admired Mrs. De Bevoise. She has not one particle of false modesty ; she will take right hold and help dress that just as though it was a finger. And W. T. delayed a long time from going his Kansas journey, because he disliked to leave G. II. B. in other M.D.'s practice to draw off his water and dress his *wound* of such public notoriety. Thus it was four months and more before Gabriel preached in the pulpit—and then but part of the day, because unable. But many of his churchmen, as well as outsiders, were discomforted and seeking his removal. Thus time wore on till winter, and " Gabriel by some mishap, report had it, fell, and broke that wound afresh, causing him, it was said, to be in danger."

In fact there was danger, for most of his people were themselves advising that he must ask for dismission. One of his church deacons told me these words : " It's no use for Mr. De Bevoise to attempt to preach here longer ; he is not going to be able to stand in the pulpit—we must have another pastor." A few weeks more only passed, and G. II. De Bevoise was told to ask dismission, or he would be dismissed without his asking. Gabriel therefore sent in his resignation, which was unanimously accepted. But some cover must be used for him ; and so his friends caused to be printed their regret at his resignation. Thus the man who hunted E. R. Hill into jail was, by an unmention-able sickness, asked by his own churchmen to resign his pastoral relations with that church in North Brookfield. For which God be praised ! He was doing more injury to orthodoxy than all the Ingersols or infidels that could be packed in said town. And I affirm it is not infidels who are killing orthodoxy. That church itself is doing the work.

In Sept., 1877, I wrote to the pastor of the Union Cong. Church, N. B., of which I had been a member since 1854, asking said church not to administer communion to S. Bothwell, who had fabricated the testimony he uttered against me Sept. 14, and praying said church to deal with him as the church covenant re-quires when a brother is offended, etc. Now see orthodox worth !

On my return from captivity some time in March, 1878, I had a letter brought to my door from said church by a little son of one of its deacons, said letter informing me that said church, Oct. 4, 1877, voted to drop my name from their church membership, for the only reason assigned, I had withdrawn myself from its communion such a length of time. (The letter is at home.) That very "sister in Christ" who had waited on, and done her part and more working to support that church, when I ought to have been in bed with my husband, was without one word, visit, or act ever from one of its members to hold me and keep me in its sacred fold—but voted to drop E. R. Hill to sink or swim without their church profession assistance. But Bothwell they cherish as a boon, and I guess it will prove the foundation of that church was truly laid by the devil, as has often been said. I ask orthodoxy to look at the above church, and see what aids and makes infidels.

In Sept., 1878, of court time, I was down to my land, the place of my birth, after some early apples. Standing upon those great doorsteps at my late father's house, I saw passing down on the railroad track twelve men on my first mowing. Nye and Luther Deland drove up to the gate a few feet from me, hitching their horse without speaking to me. I said to them : "What are all these men down here looking my land over for ?" Luther speaks : " What are you down here for ?" Mrs. H. : " I am here, sir, on my own property, attending to my own business (I had a large basket of apples in my hands), and you, sirs, are trespassers on my property. It is a great pity you both could not be back in

the poor out-of-the-way sunken holes you were born and brought
up in. But such is life." Reader, those men were down again
to appraise my R. R. damage, as they had said it should be settled this term of court. But I wrote to court to have said case
put over, as my important witness was not in the United States.
But I made every effort to get settlement without court after my
terrible false imprisonment. Knowing from that plot no justice
would be done me, I wrote letters offering to settle said claim at
great sacrifice.

My brother Moses, at this homestead, was at this time sued
by Bacon, Hopkins & Bacon, for their services in his railroad
suit; the homestead attached for sheriff's sale by L. P. Deland.
That advertisement caused me to go and rescue my brother
M., by paying said B. H. & B.'s bill and expenses, thus stopping
said sale, which maddened Warren Tyler and his sister, as I
have been told, more than anything else I ever did. They have
not spoken or looked at me if they could avoid it since.

Before that sale was pulled down, Bothwell posted up another
sheriff's sale of said homestead for taxes. I knew those taxes
were paid. I was present at their payment, for I was just in
from the cemetery from seeing the little stone placed at babies'
grave. Upon the top is Willie, Albert (little darlings), Warren, Walter. Upon the side is my prayer : "Tread softly ! The
ground is holy. See whose grave she weepeth o'er ! Lo ! the simple
superscription : Little Darlings—nothing more." I went to the
home kitchen. Moses and Bothwell were counting the money to
pay those taxes, and I saw Bothwell write a receipt. I started at
once for the press and told them and Bothwell not to let that
sale be posted again. Those taxes were paid, and would not
be paid the second time. If Bothwell could have annihilated
me he would done it then ; but his force was on the wane. I
sought my brother. He knew he had paid his taxes, but could
not find receipt, and Bothwell had not checked his name in the
tax book. I said to my brother, M. : "Don't you stop looking
for that receipt till you find it. It is in this house somewhere."
I went home. In a few days my brother found his receipt, and
thus Bothwell was prevented collecting those taxes a second
time for his own pocket. And thus you see Bothwell had less
money to aid that church !

The reader must pardon these items, for the last pages of this book will show why they were written. And a few days more pass, and my brother, M. is sued again by Flynn, whose wife figures as "Eve." Said Flynn worked for my brother, one haying season, my brother paying the wife and husband money, farm products, use of horse and carriage—overpaying said Flynn's wages, but no settlement ; and that modern wife (Eve) meant to get the whole over again and more.

I went over with my brother before Justice Duel, not expecting any hearing, as the time of work sued for and all was false, as my brother could show. But on reaching said office, there sat L. C. Barnes, Esq., Flynn and wife, and J. Duncan. My brother had no book account, only items, time when paying, etc. Barnes opened the case for Flynn, stating the year of said work, etc. I objected, as Flynn did not work for my brother that year. Barnes immediately says : "I mean such year. I repeat the warrant of bill entered for suit ; affirm otherwise," which Justice Duel gave Tyler. But the case went on—Flynn's wife denying generally. When Flynn came to be sworn, I said : " Flynn, think what it is to take a false oath ! " The man turned death pale and reeled. But Barnes prompted him. But my cross-questions brought out the truth, and proved the payments had been made. And what do you think ? Barnes ruled thus : "Mrs. Hill's questions were not directed to the Court, but drew from the plaintiff answers he did not mean ! And the Court must rule in favor of Flynn, because Tyler has no book account. And I want the Court to hurry up its decision, as I want to get out of this." And Duel give Barnes his wish, against true evidence, just because Moses Tyler had not his account written in a book. Oh ! on what a slender thread some things hang.

My brother went over in a few days and paid some twenty dollars or more, leaving unpaid less than ten dollars of that justice court demand ! Justice Duel telling Tyler to be sure, after this, to have a book account.

That others were in troubled waters from and by people who wish to obtain what does not by right or title belong to them, showing also the ruling spirit in North Brookfield, at this De Bevoise, Bates, and others, railroad notoriety Little b. m. Nye is now figuring by his acts above law, except his own making. And thus attempts in the summer of 1879, to take from a war widow, Nichols, land her husband had owned by deed over thirty years; said land adjoining an estate of B. M. Nye's nieces. Said Nye was also filching for land the property of the town. Mrs. Nichols had removed her front yard fence, leaving only the posts. B. M. Nye is surveyor, and he went right into that front yard, tramping down flowers, placing his assumed boundaries to take part of said yard, also cutting off the drive way to Nichol's barn—thus involving said war widow Nichols in a lawsuit to defend her legally owned real estate. Nye's nieces, by his order, proceeded to draw stone to build a wall, as Nye saw fit to make a boundary. But the Batcheller shoe manufactory had a gang of men who took up the case, in order to save the war widow Nichols' real estate to her without the expense of modern courts. Said wall was being laid, when, lo! one night some hundred men, with yoke of oxen, stone boats, and horse power, dragged off every stone, and tipped them, as it was said, into a mud pond! Nye was going to prosecute. Prosecute who?

Nye ordered more stones to be drawn, for his nieces' wall should be built, as he said. The big, heavy stones were again piled there, and again the night force came out and dragged every stone there placed into that mud pond pit!

There has been no wall attempt since.

Thus B. M. Nye was subdued, and the widow saved in her right without the modern court taking all she had or more to save her from B. M. Nye's lawlessness. I ask, candidly, if it is not high time that courts are reformed, and thus give citizens their rights which are now taken as robbers in high positions see fit, they knowing the defendants cannot and have not money to be used in courts for their defence.

Before the building of the N. B. R. R., in 1875, which made debt upon said town of five per cent. of her valuation, there had been great demand for more school room. The largest number of the citizens being Irish, sending most scholars to our schools, that nationality wanted school-houses located in their vicinity, in said North Brookfield village, which was overruled for fear of their creed, which was most unjust. Therefore sundry places were sought for school room, also an engine house, with the modern perquisites was needed. The firemen did not think the basement of our high school-house a suitable place for them to meet and keep their fire apparatus. Their argument was: " Build engine-house and thus make two school-rooms in that basement." Furthermore, they wanted a new engine and more hose, and so forth. I will add, the need of more men of brains, too. Time wore on, and every town warrant would have those articles in it, which would be wrangled over till floored, for we could not build till more of our railroad debt is paid. The wrangle was kept up severely till one May morning in 1878, about High School-hour time, the fire-alarm sounds that High School building is on fire from basement to attic. The fire was such, the engine and hose could not be got out. The Batcheller Shoe Manufactory sending out their fire apparatus till joined by neighboring towns, whose aid did not reach us to be of service. Thus in less than two hours that school building, with its new chemical apparatus, maps, portraits, and piano, and all the scholars' books; were in ashes. Save a few timbers ! Therefore a town warrant was posted to call a meeting in seven days to find or build school-room and build engine-house, purchase engine, hose, and all other necessary items, and furnish scholars with new books. Oh! the fire was thought to have caught near the furnace, near some chemicals somewhat combustible, for the school-house was locked! My pen will fail to describe that town meeting, but Bates was going to have a chance to be very efficient. He would attend to any business and give service in this emergency. And Bates did. Town meetings were often held to consider school building and engine-house plans, and costs of construction, and where to locate. In one of those wrangling meetings, Dr. Warren Tyler, who had been selectman during the past ten years (but had been dropped from that office at last April Town Meeting), spoke of the towns trying to get lease of a large three-story, unoccupied shoe shop, within ten rods of the burnt High School building, thus giving more school room than we had before the fire, and at small expense compared with cost of a new house.

Reader, the hissing and shouts of " Sit down," with hiss, at his most every sentence, was the scene. Warren Tyler, M.D., with every muscle twitching in his face (like the morning of March 3), replies to them : " This damned rabble of poll-tax payers and few others may hiss and shout till hell freezes over. I shall not be stopped nor set down by this hissing pack, who are having our town's property destroyed, to get buildings that they vote to build out of their poll-tax money, with few others as our railroad got birth. The same rabble want to get three per cent. of our valuation in a debt for a school house and appurtenances, and three per cent. more for engine-house and equipments; and it is high time this expense is stopped; and these meetings ought to be filled with men who have the burden to carry. I want school-room, and suitable rooms. When I was a boy the school-rooms were twenty-five feet square, with sixty and seventy scholars in attendance in winter, and in summer same ratio. These scholars were scholars, and have made and been our most honest, useful men and women. This rabble that is moved in here don't own anything but a few puny young ones that hardly know enough to go into the house out of the rain. They must have the most modern city-styled school-houses for their ninnies; and the vote of every sensible man must be cast against this rabble-determined, superfluous debt." . . . During the summer the town built, under Bates & Co., a High School house upon the old stand, with six large school rooms, third floor High School room, with all appurtenances thereunto belonging; and also one large Engine-house, two stories high, equipped with new engine, hose, fire extinguisher, dressing-room, meeting-room, furnished off in style which must have exceeded their most sanguine expectations.

During these days of town excitement I was busy trying to get my barn ruins removed, and my strength, of which I had been shorn. Just before the sitting of the Superior Court, in September, I received a letter from Gile, Esq , who obtained my release from captivity, stating that I must come to Worc. to make preparations for my case against the N. B. R. R. Co. I had told said Gile that *if I needed counsel in said case in Worc. I should like his services.*

I went to Worc., to see the records and make ready to have my case put over, etc. On entering the Clerk's room there stood Esquire Nelson, R. R. Defts. counsel Hopkins, and also Gile. I readily saw they were making arrangements, etc., as it might please Defts., as heretofore. The Clerk gave me my R. R. documents to copy, those gentlemen passing out. I said to Nelson I hoped to be able to get settlement with the R. R. Def'ts., He replied : "I should have done that years ago," in his biting way of speaking. I saw then in his spirit just what I wanted to find out.

On opening the warrants I found Bacon, Hopkins & Bacon, Gile & Merrill, counsel on said case. I had written Bacon, Hopkins & Bacon in July, 1877, telling them I did not desire their services longer in my R. R. case (as Stoddard, King, Whitings, Kittredge, had all counselled said firm in regard to their railroad claims, each party withdrawing from their arbitration). Bates & Nye, R. R. Defts., "would speak with their friends of what P. C. Bacon and Col. Hopkins told them," making those parties and myself feel as if those attorneys were riding two horses. The horses were going in different directions; therefore the R. R. plaintiff's horse left those attorneys with the defendants' horse. Col. Hopkins replying in severest manner to me also, stating the firm *withdraw from my R. R. case*, and further counsel from them I could not have in any way. That was the reason of my letters and telegrams to Worc. Court, etc., to put over my case.

I wrote to Judge Aldrich in December, 1877, when at 62 Brooklyn Heights, to put over my case, as it was impossible by letter or telegram to get one word as to my lawsuits pending. No answer. The last time I met Judge Aldrich was at the American Teachers' Institute at Montpelier, Vt. From said place I went to White Mountains, July, 1877, and I thought the Judge a friend. Judge Aldrich did advise B., H. & B. to attend to my R. R. case in my absence, as Col. Hopkins told me after the same day of my meeting those men in the Clerk's room at Worc. My thanks to Judge P. E. A. for that humane act. . . . I also tried to find Henry Bacon, of that firm, said day, about my bank book, which had been kept from me when I presented it for payment, etc., in August, 1877, said H. B. making minutes of the same. I was told H. B. was stopping at Hartford. Every time I went to Worc. it was tedious. The very name of Worc. Courts will ever breed disgust, contempt, because of their illegal persecutions of me, E. R. Hill.

Therefore I determined that, even at great sacrifice and loss, I would get my R. R. claims settled before December Court. I verbally applied to R. R. Directors for said claim to be settled. No notice. I then wrote offers of settlement, which were replied to as follows:

NORTH BROOKFIELD, August 29, 1878.

MRS. ELIZABETH R. HILL:

Dear Madam—Your letter of even date, to the President and Directors of the North Brookfield Railroad Co. was delivered at once to the President, who, on reading it, and being informed that you expressed a wish that it might, if possible, be considered before the regular meeting next Saturday evening, called a special meeting this evening, at which, after discussion, it was voted to *reject* your offer to deed the land in controversy for the sum of seven hundred dollars. In the absence of the Secretary, the writer was appointed to communicate to you the action of the Board on the subject.

Very respectfully,
CHAS. ADAMS, JR.

NORTH BROOKFIELD, Sept. 3, 1878.

MRS. E. R. HILL, North Brookfield, Mass.:

Madam—I am instructed by the Directors of the North Brookfield Railroad Company to inform you that your proposition to settle your claims against this company, as made this day, is respectfully rejected.

THEODORE C. BATES,
Clerk of the Directors of the No. B. R. R. Co.

My last personal attempt was at a meeting of the Railroad Directors, Saturday evening last, before the first Tuesday in December, 1878. There were present, T. C. Bates, B. M. Nye, Alden Bacheller, Freeman Walker, Chas. Adams, Jr., G. C. Lincoln; and E. R. Hill was in their presence alone, asking *those* men who had taken my land, my liberty, and tried their mightiest to blacken my character (reader, have you ever read Ivanhoe? If so, see me as "Isaac and Rebekah,") to give me the sum of $550 (not one quarter pay for my damage to my property.) Nye refused quickly. I then said will you settle for $500. Defts., No! I said no such offer came from me, as pay for my land; it was to end the quarrel; they had my land and my labor and trouble during the building of that railroad; and my terrible sufferings from their imprisoning me since gives you this very small sum to pay if you will. Freeman Walker says, "I know you have had to suffer." The expression of Chas. Adams, Jr., so hard and relentless (but I have seen the same look in C. A., Jr., since, in the North Brookfield Ladies' Library quarrel with the town); T. C. Bates' eye I could not catch, neither would he seek proposal direct to me, but through Nye or Walker; Bacheller was silent; G. C. Lincoln would look at me with a boyish laugh, as if it were fun. The only offer I could get that eve was made, to give the Commissioners award with simple interest to date.

I rose to leave the room, saying, if they should conclude to pay the small sum I had offered to receipt, I would like to have them do so and save me the trouble of going to Worc. to answer to my case when called on the list for trial next Tuesday. Chas. Adams, Jr., replied, "You can go to Worc., for we shall not make you another offer," with tone and look that covered even his words with muck. Tuesday I went down to court. The Clerk told me he would see my case answered "for trial," when called. My case on the list for trial was the thirty-ninth; Clerk also saying he would write me when to come down for trial. Nye said to me, "Esq. Nelson said the case was first on the list to be tried, and it would be tried first." I did not demur, but coolly said the plaintiff was ready, be it first or last.

WORCESTER, MASS., Dec. 11, 1878.
Mrs. Elizabeth R. Hill, North Brookfield, Mass., No. 1955, will be in order to-morrow.

JOHN A. DANA, Clerk.

I had my own blood cousin, Stilman Dane, to accompany me to court and carry my parcels, and a very intelligent man. Dewey is on the bench, who had been my counsel, and had ever treated me with great esteem. Soon came in Hopkins, plain seen moves, and queries, "Who or where is Mrs. Hill's counsel?" Reader, I was fully prepared to meet my case. As my case was not likely to be reached that A.M., I passed into the waiting room. In comes defendant's counsel, Nelson, and says, "Mrs. Hill, I hear you have offered to settle thus and so. I have just told the railroad defendant   I shall charge them $150 to try the case, and I am going to have this case disposed of," and goes right on figuring so and so. "I will pay you $650, and you must give deed." Mr. Dane says, "Take it," and I did.

When Esquire Nelson drew the deed Nye had informed him the railroad was five rods wide. On his reading said deed I said: "Please *insert eighty feet* for that five rods, as the profile of railroad claims." Nelson then gave Nye a biting query: "Why did you state five rods to me? We've got all this to write over now!" I had *then* an internal smile. At the N. B. depot stood Chas. Adams, Jr., and Mr. Montague, waiting the return of railroad President, B. M. Nye, from that *court* (and not one other person sent down as railroad defendant to that *to be court*). The train comes, and B. M. Nye and E. R. II are on the platform. Chas. A., Jr., and Mr. Montague lock arms with B. M. Nye, and walk off, with bent listening ear to know which, how, or when. Mrs. E. R. II. goes off lone to her sacred cottage home. All silently I enter. No welcoming hand greets me; but methinks I hear their gentle whispers floating in the ambient air. Home comforts! how pure, how sacred! Next morning, before 8 o'clock, B. M. Nye is at my residence to pay E. R. II. the $650 and take that deed. When I handed that deed I said, "That deed is given and was signed on the same ground that Whittlesy gave up the keys to the Northampton bank robbers. Father—mother—Almighty God! witness this unjust obtained deed!" And my tears flowed, and will ever well up from my heart at being compelled to surrender to robbery of land, liberty of speech, because its robbers are protected by forms (to the ignorant) called law. But no comments were heralded by the press only "Settlement had been made with E. R. Hill for land taken by N. B. R. R. Co., said company paying $650." Of course, with some of it was laughable to think after all defendant's threats, E. R. Hill, single-handed, had won the case. But revenge is what the N. B. R. R. Co. are manifesting in their every move toward E. R. II.

Readers, there is not on earth a person who desires to see progress and the public interest promoted, and all in harmony with statute law and divine command more than E. R. II, whom that mob viciously continue to persecute. Many are the changes in our midst. The wheel of time rolls on, bringing the

" first, last—and the last, first." Mr. Clay was a superior High School teacher for a number of terms in our town before the burning of said H. S. B., and after. But he, too, was envied. I never could see for what, reader, but his superiority and efficiency as a teacher. But he had to succumb, and leave for another school field, which gave him $1,800 instead of $1,500. Said Clay had incited in the spirit of his scholars the creed of a free public library and reading room, which many citizens had agitated, but were always defeated with, " We cannot have such a public expense added to our already burdened taxpayers." But the High School scholars gave public exhibitions, and, by solicitation, obtained some $500, and caused an article to be inserted in town warrant, April, 1879, asking the town to furnish a free public reading room, and for donations for a free public library, which T. C. Bates most effectually aided by giving $500, E. A. Batcheller $1,000, Mr. Montague, $400, and others smaller sums. Thus those small beginnings were being consummated, and nothing remained but to find a suitable place for their library and reading room, which the money donated would purchase. Then up rose the North Brookfield Ladies' Library Association, which was formed in 1869, and by membership fees, sociables, exhibitions, and fairs, they had accumulated about 1,100 volumes. Citizens were privileged to take out books from said N. B. L. L. A. if they could pay $2 per year. That association was popular with the few, and when they found a free public library and reading room was going to be established at once, the N. B. L. L. A. presented their library to the town as a free public library, calling a town meeting to consider and accept the gift.

As T. C. Bates was chairman and chief man against (this tongue war, for such it was), B. M. Nye, Chas. Adams, Jr., W. Tyler, G. H. De Be., and others, who were such active enemies to E. R. H., were now being held down by Bates and his force. The town voted to accept the N. B. L. L., but it was to be in rank secondary to the new purchased library by T. C. Bates and others. The N. B. L. L. A. were so offended they withdrew their offer if their library could not stand in historical archives as the first established T. F. P. L. in N. B. ! ! In every town warrant N. B. L. L. A. would have an article about their library, and its rights were advocated by those men who saw plainly if that library was not first in name neither would they ever have control of the new library. Thus great delays were made in the purchase of our library, not knowing but some books would thus be duplicated if purchase was made before the proffered gifts were in the town's custody. Meeting after meeting, wrangle upon wrangle, which should be first in that library. In another town warrant the N. B. L. L. A. had an article giving that library the second time, with some worded change in presentation, and Bates had the town's acceptance as before; and such small selfishness as was exhibited by C. A., Jr., and W. T., and others, over that library! If it had been on the auction block it would not have sold for $500 (nor half that, it was said). Those very men were wrangling most disgracefully over their labor in purchasing their proffered gift, and not one among them had paid out five dollars from their own purse for those books.

During those wrangles I sat a listener (*never* REPORTING, for the quarrel, truthfully stated, would have disgraced South Sea Islanders), and drew parallels between what those men had taken from me worth thousands of dollars, and see how they quarrel over that *munificent gift* of 1,000 *volumes*, the largest half—two-thirds—wore out. After the town voted this second time to accept that proffered gift, W. T., M.D., rose and said: "The town has voted to accept our library, but you have not got it yet;" and unyielding remarks came from C. Adams, Jr., with same face and manner he a few months before bestowed upon the lone widow and fatherless. Rev. Hewes spoke, I heard, repeatedly, "that man ought to be took and put in a lock-up every time he speaks here." On going out of the hall I heard "that library shall be given in *ashes* before it shall be placed second to the other." Therefore said N. B. L. L. A. withdrew their proffered gift the second time, and soon after donated and sent said books to Berea College, Berea, Kentucky. When it was reported to me the N. B. L. L. was thus donated and gone, I said: "Believing, I rejoice to know that quarrel is removed." The North Brookfield Free Public Library and Reading Room was first opened to the public November 26, 1879. I was at the opening, and I thought this new institution would contribute most effectually to aid and encourage our youth to obtain useful knowledge. The Free Public Library department was not opened to the public until April 1, 1880. I was the first there. Both rooms are open to the public every afternoon and evening in the year, except Sunday, the library containing two thousand or more volumes, and no place was more gratifying to me than to see the young and old deeply absorbed in reading the newspapers, periodicals, and magazines as I frequented our Free Public Reading Room and Library.

A most notable fact, these men and theirs who were members of the late N. B. L. L. A. are not ever present. And I know it has been a great annoyance to that late Association that I was in full fellowship with this new, great advantageous institution, not favoring that selfish N. B. L. L. A.

My barn walls stand a monument still. In September, 1880, I employed Peter Carter & Brother to build an "L" to my house, giving me wood-house and other rooms that were finished off my lost barn. My house was repainted and varnished in every part. I bought all the timber, windows, and paint. Every item used I negotiated and paid for, making my sacred home doubly dear. In fact it almost seemed hard to go from my house even on a day trip to Worcester, where I purchased my windows and blinds, and also trying to get my bank-book which was taken from me in August, 1877. Said book I obtained in 1861 by investing seventy-five dollars in Foster Street Savings Bank, and had taken out twenty-five dollars and interest, this fifty dollars remaining since 1863. In 1874 a mortgage was paid I held of $1,100. I left the same with P. C. Bacon, Esq, to invest in such savings bank as he thought best. Said B. invested $500 in this same bank on Foster street. I did not think then nor after anything about it, as my other book had laid away to accumulate for other purposes. That time came, I presented my bank book and it was taken and kept, the man saying: "We never give two books." I said I had two, P. C. Bacon getting my last. Those bank robbers have my book and money yet. The man who kept my bank book has since hung himself.

I have repeatedly made demands for my bank book. Henry Deland and D. Whiting often telling me there were so many ways in which the bank could manipulate, I would be best off to let it go. But there is, and ever will be, a determination on my part to get my money out of that bank. I went to P. C.

Bacon the very hour of its being taken and told him the case. He was very excited at its rehearsal and nervously said: "You are always in a fuss. I can't do anything about it! It will cost you thrice as much to get it as its value. You *versus* that bank! You can't do anything!" His son Henry came in, saying, "What's up?" I told him. He put on his hat and said: "I'll go with you and make minutes," and he did. And then he says to me: "You write to the directors of said bank." I did, and here is their reply:

WORCESTER COUNTY INSTITUTION FOR SAVINGS,
WORCESTER, MASS., AUGUST 21, 1877.

MRS. E. R. HILL, North Brookfield:

Your application in relation to a deposit book claimed by you was placed before the Board of Investment at their meeting last evening. The Board believe that the books of the institution afford conclusive evidence of the payment of the deposit to you, and instruct me to notify you that they decline to accede to the request contained in your communication to them of the 14th inst. Very respectfully,

J. HENRY HILL,
Secretary Worcester Co. Ins. for Savings.

After my captivity I went into Foster Street S. Bank and called for my book, taking John Gilman with me as witness. Calling for my book, an old man there, by name of Hamilton, would not produce it, till Gilman says : "I wish to see it. I have always known Mrs. Hill, and I never knew her in any way but the most upright, steadfast woman I ever knew." Hamilton smirkingly said: "The papers don't say so." Gilman says: "What has been said in the papers are lies, and I demand to see that book and books with Mrs. Hill." Hamilton brought my book and theirs, showing to Gilman. Gilman saw at once figures *looked as* if tampered with, and to me it was plain as my nose on my face. I have been there twice since—the last time the first week in February, 1881—telling them I should at once bring suit if said bank did not pay me in full. They smilingly said, "We have no time now." Hamilton died alone, shortly after his insult to me before Gilman. Thus one bankman hung himself, and the other died suddenly. My counsel was ready to bring suit the week I was obliged to leave my sacred home, and said counsel said he would get every cent due me in that bank. And Almighty God help me to get it yet is my prayer. Bates at this time had obtained the position of bank director in Worcester; and a bank president of the First National in Worcester is under great disgrace with woman *vs.* wife. Pond was one other great bank thief in Worcester, but he is in State prison for twenty, more or less, years; and may all such get retribution!

T. C. Bates is about thirty-six or thirty-seven years of age, son of Elijah Bates, mechanic, who died some twenty years since. A hard-working man, and all of his family were notorious for the great amount of shoe-closing performed by this family of thirteen or eighteen children. Their shoe-closing gave more notoriety than other families, because in their great worldliness and haste they would send in lots of shoes with their counters and sidings part closed. In those days shoes were closed in clamps or at shoe-bench with awl and waxed thread. The father busy in making tables, stands, and coffins, in a two-story shop. Wealth, of course, rolled up from labor, and the father, who had, during the birth of all those children, lived in a very small, red one-story house, removed that house to where it now stands, and built a two-story house, which they occupied a few years—and lo! so many shavings scattered around in all directions, that house caught fire (by accident) and was burned to the ground. E. B. rebuilds better than before, and the second house in a few years, by some kind of accident, is burned. E. B. rebuilds again, each time upon the same stand, and each time a better, more commodious house, and it still stands in T. C. Bates' name. The small barn of said Elijah Bates was also burned, but this fire happened to take place during a thunder storm, and report had it, "burned by lightning." A very nice barn was rebuilt by E. Bates, which is now standing. That mechanic coffin shop of E. Bates also caught fire, and was burned to the ground, and has never been (needed) or replaced. T. C. Bates now has new gates and drive roads made in the late Bates' woods, making a place of pleasure resort just back of the residence. T. C. Bates is now the ring-leader of N. B. "The boys" know just what B. and his subordinates want done, and it is done. Thirty years ago, North Brookfield, Mass., with its old citizens, was distinguished for its educational, moral, religious, straitforward, doing unto others as you would be done by.

Then N. B. had a minister, Dr. Thomas Snell, who preached and lived daily the precepts and examples of Christ, and Rev. Christopher Cushing and Rev. Wm. H. Beecher. Those three men were ministers of the Gospel. They are gone. Our fathers, our mothers, those noble men are gone, are all gone. Not even their mantle spirit rests there, but in a few places those pure "bloods" are now few indeed.

They must not even be known if the modern citizens or mob conspirators wish them out of the way. Or if the pure blood *live on land* of their fathers, and the modern citizens want it, without money or without price, all to be done is to get some new excitement breezing. And the "modern boys" and (they will carry the ballot-box in number) their leader will take land pews, oust out every one who is in quiet enjoyment of their own legal rights, if it is thus desired by their leaders. New Braintree, East Brookfield, South Brookfield, Spencer, and West Brookfield, said towns bounding us on all sides. Those towns have had immense property destroyed by "incendiaries," and seldom has there been found the fire-bugs. The past year North Brookfield has been drinking that fire cup. I will mention one which to human beings was sad indeed. In December, 1880, the barn, 100 feet by 60, of the late Erastus Hill, who died in January, 1878, aged 69—a wealthy citizen of the old blood—a staunch opposer of the men of N. B. R. R. (illegal birth), was burned to the ground with some thirteen head of cattle, hay, and farming tools, just after sunset. No clue to who did it, but as its location was where smoking abounds, it was thought the great probability was an accident. The barn was the property of his son-in-law, fortunately well insured. Then comes one Sabbath, and Mr. K.'s two barns and their contents are burned to the ground, between North Brookfield and Spencer. Now comes Arthur Knight's livery stable right close to our Town House and Free Public Reading Room and Library. (I will interpolate our Town Hall public building has been burned three times in the last twenty-five years, and in one of those fires all of our public and historical records were consumed. And to-day those records of my birth, school teaching, and marriage, and the births of my three first children and other citizens of my young days and

of our fathers, were mingled in those ashes. Oh ! the scenes of
my childhood, how I love thee!) But the fire was put out at
9 P.M., for a great snowstorm was raging, with our new engine
and fire extinguisher; the flames were subdued without burning or
smoking our Free Public Reading Room and Library—had that
barn burned down, that library and reading-room would have
been smoked, soaked. Yes, our greatest public good would have
been ruined. (I speak of that library as our greatest blessing
for young and old, and I mean it.) Those three churches (orthodox), with those ministers of late years—what are they ? I ask,
what? I give an example of their "seed-sowing." Rev.
Hird, pastor of Union Cong. Church in N. B., heard of E. R. H.
and her book, and sent to borrow one to read, etc. After reading said book he called church meetings (as report told me) ;
but Rev. Hird was silenced, etc. Rev. Hird sent word to
E. R. H. that I had his sympathies, but his hands were tied. I
smile—don't you? Rev. Hird has not ever called on me since.

Again the fire fiend is out. "Tho. Snell's (son of the late Rev.
Dr. T. Snell,) barn is burned to the ground—part insured."
Whose moonshine was that barn in? Now comes "Widow A.
Stoddard's barn and all therein, burned to the ground—insured."
Then comes the late " Wm. Whiting's barn which is burned; but
the occupant saved his cattle." The papers still bring: " Failed
attempts to burn C. P. Adams's store and box shop. There
were bundles of shavings filled with kerosene found; some were
on fire;" who wants different buildings? Next comes " an attempt
to burn the First Congregational Church. A bag of shavings
filled with kerosene was hung between the window and blinds.
They caught this *specie* of a man thirty years old. He denied it
till after being in the lock-up fifteen hours—he confessed it was
his work, but he was not going to set it fire—he only did it to
get up a sensation. He was a member of that church and—its
janitor." Next paper—"The Town's Custom House is burned
with all its storage. The merchants *well* insured." What was
the matter with that Custom House? Next comes the two story
new school house in Dist. No. 1, " set on fire, but saved with little
damage, the fire being timely seen." Who wanted that altered
or removed? The " small buildings I have not mentioned." The
above incidents in North Brookfield I found at Rowell's news
room. Such vandalism, outlaw, perjury, blackmail, slander,

rampant in my native town ! ! ! Oh, what a curse ! Are there not righteous ones enough left to redeem that modern Sodom of sin ?

L. E. Barnes, Esq., by petition of H. Green, was appointed guardian of a chronic insane widow of the late Horace Green, who died of paralysis in 1879. L. E. Barnes will wax fat in his new rich prospectus, as he may quirk the law. It has been often remarked of his legal ability, " That his mental capacity was far more fitted for his hen business of producing eggs for market, of marvelous size," as the papers inform us. Now that widow's farm of more than 200 acres will give him a nice chance to get fowls and hunt into every nest to find eggs of some description. When, lo ! he finds that note of the late Green held against M. Tyler. Said lost note had been paid, etc. Green and Tyler were both farmers and great friends—always trading and dealing in their needs in the most friendly manner. Leonard Warren settled the late Green's estate, finding said lost note. L. Warren accordingly presented said note to M. Tyler, finding it had been paid—and that H. Green's estate was in debt to M. Tyler, said L. Warren, adm., telling M. Tyler to bring in his account. M. Tyler neglects, and L. Warren makes return of said Green's estate settled.

Afterwards, Barnes, Esq., is guardian by a nephew's wish. Barnes now hunts every nest, his hand grasps the $50 note egg. He seeks Madam Flynn, and unites that unpaid court demand of $8 with this egg note of $50, and forthwith sues M. Tyler, and the homestead is posted again for Sheriff's sale, Feb. 26, 1881, by Luther P. Deland. The advertisement our first information. I wrote Deland & Barnes at once, challenging " the sale of the homestead," as said real estate was not owned by M. Tyler at all; said Tyler had sold and given deed of said homestead more than a year since. Also, if Madam Flynn had claim against M. Tyler I hope she would at once seek M. Tyler and have friendly settlement. For there was no chance to collect from that homestead. Also, giving notice if Warren Tyler wanted the money on his mortgage upon said homestead, E. R. Hill will gladly cancel the same. I then personally called on L. E. Barnes to find what constituted his Flynn claim against M. Tyler. He referred me to the court for papers. I told him to explain and save me the trouble of going over to South Brookfield. He would not. I told him I feared Warren Tyler and H. P. Bartlett were interested in this suit, as Warren has ever wished to get control of the homestead, though not a child in the world; but two boys bear his name in full, both boys being of epileptic and lunatic descent. I told Barnes if W. T. had not made any inquiry of that sale, the reason was plain. And Esq. Barnes, I repeat to you, I would be glad to cancel W. Tyler's mortgage on said homestead and thus relieve Warren of any more anxiety. "I see," says Barnes, " you are full of money, and you are not taxed anything either. Ready to pay the Dr.'s mortgage." And I said: "The one whom I did business for would furnish the money." B: "Nobody will believe that, and I am going to have you taxed hereafter." Hill: " I solemnly swear my property stands on valuation at higher value than any man's real estate on Elm street. And I am willing to be taxed as others, upon oath; and rejoice in the privilege of paying the widow's mite towards maintaining our Free Public Library and Reading room, and decorating the soldiers' graves," which said Barnes was noted for being against as illegal to decorate those soldiers' graves. And he was not willing to be taxed for it, etc. Barnes, W. Tyler, Bartlett, were in commotion, going to Worcester often, and an ax was evidently grinding.

Mr. Chas. Kittredge sued the Town of North Brookfield in September, 1880, for their illegal railroad taxation. The waves began to heave, and vengence was written on the brows of those men who were to be defendants. Whenever I met any of said body, their look was "crush." I asked the meaning? When told the above, I said: Mr. or Mrs. K. have not mentioned that to be for a year or more. Bates and Nye interviewing Kittredge's counsel (Hopkins & Briggs), asking them if they really meant suit, etc. Bates saying, "as report has it:" " He did not suppose there was a lawyer in Massachusetts who would bring that case against us." This railroad grudge is now issued in full force on E. R. Hill. We must get her out of the way. Mrs. Hill out of the way, we will dispose of Kittredge without gloves. She is their hope (which was not true). The plot is being deftly marked out as in 1877 by the same conspirators. Mrs. Hill had beautified her home, was living in full enjoyment of its many sacred comforts. And more, she is in her fruition of happiness in that Library—storing up knowledge (it had been said). That mob had till this time thought E. R. H· dead - minus decomposition.

Friday, Feb. 11, 1881.—I called again at Barnes' "law office," he was not present. I wrote on postal card and left at P. O., asking for interview with Barnes at 5 P.M. I then called at L. P. Deland's, and found out some facts of that "to be sale." In returning I called at Barnes' abode—saw his wife. Mrs. B. saying her husband had gone to Worcester, but would return on 4:30 train. As I arrived at depot the train comes in. (Said depot is 60 rods perhaps from my sacred home.) Barnes and Tyler, M.D., step out of the cars in haste. I said to the agent, "Speak to Esq. Barnes" agent calls Barnes—"A lady *here* wishes to see you." B. turns, sees E. R. H., heads round, rushing off to Post Office. As I arrived at P. O. Barnes was coming out. I said : "Esq. Barnes, I wish to consult with you a few moments about that Flynn suit." Barnes replies in the most boorish manner thus : "Ge-go-go long—go way." E. R. H. repeats : "Go long—go way." Is that all the two-legged species can say ?

Feb. 12.—I went to Boston on legal *bank* business. Returning I stopped at Worcester to see Hopkins and Briggs, Attorneys. Their office was closed; therefore I went to Hon. E. B. Stoddard's, Esq., showing the homestead deed (not recorded), and telling Stoddard I should take out a writ of review for my brother, and thus stop that sheriff's sale, as Madam Flynn and H. Green's estate were in debt some $100 and more to M. Tyler, and if Barnes could dig up dead bones the same was Tyler's privilege. As I went into E. B. S.'s office Adin Thayer, probate judge, passed out. Stoddard was very anxious in his manner, causing me to ask why ? S. says I am thinking how much you have to see to and how they act with you, and says, I advise you to come down soon and make preparations against that sale." I told S. I should come Monday 14th. I did. On my return stopped at East Brookfield, and was carried by private team to Justice Duel's, South Brookfield, by C. H. Forbes, completing my arrangements for taking out "Writ of Review," for my brother M., arriving at my own residence 6 P.M. Most pleasantly everything greets me in this my sacred resting place on earth. I sat enjoying my many most cosy comforts and reading

my newspapers till most ten o'clock. My door bell *rings ! ! !*
An uncommon event at that hour ! ! ! " One never knows what
sudden blow lies veiled in innocent blue of sky; and fate is
ambushed Indian foe that creeps through calm and stillness
nigh ; and sometimes swift misfortunes come with sandled feet
and muffled drum: the foe are crowding, stealthy serpents creep,
preparing spring, and venomous leap, to *snatch* at *freedom* in
our care as vipers creep from everglade to sting our children in
the shade ! ! !"

My door bell again rings hurriedly; I ask " Who is at my
door ?" the reply comes in low tones: " A friendly messenger
—let me in quick ! " I open a wide entrance. The friend says:
" Mrs. Hill, I come here to let you know a damnable plot is laid
to stop you life here *in this town*." I ask: " *what do you mean ?* "
Reply: " Do as I tell you—it is your only safety from the plot
of F. T. Blackmer and L. E. Barnes and others. , You must not
remain in this house till morning, for F. T. Blackmer, Esq.,
Worcester, has applied to Probate Court (Adin Thayer, judge)
to have you forthwith committed to the Insane Asylum in Worcester. Barnes had made oath to the papers this evening, and
said Barnes, after making oath to said papers Feb. 14, 8 P.M.,
1881, was asked: " What are you doing that for?" Answer
Barnes: " Mrs. Hill has been down to Ben Butler, Boston, to
bring suit against F. T. Blackmer, Esq., for what he said of
Mrs. Hill in Donahue's Court—*for which she ought to be hung,*
and think of her trying to stop my sheriff sale—but we will stop
her at once, and have no more annoyance from her in law
courts or anywhere else. Two M. D.'s are coming from Worcester on the 7:30 A.M. train, to see Mrs. Hill as soon as out of
bed, and we will have her in the Asylum before noon to-
morrow."

"All plans are now made, but just getting the body of E. R.
Hill ; and she will not get out again as she did before, and Dr.
Tyler says Mrs. Hill has annoyed him and the town long enough.
We shall have her sure to-morrow, for they say she has a ter-
rible cold, and will not be likely to be from home to-morrow.
That is my haste." And Barnes goes off with his perjured war-
rant with exultation. Reader, I still breathe after that most
terrible of all plots being told me. A pause at length. I said:
" Is it possible I have again got to leave my sacred home, so

pure, so fresh and new, which at this time my cup of happiness was replete in its new comforts? and have I again got to leave all to that malignant mob in ambush?" Oh! Almighty God, what is Thy purpose? Thou sendest me this messenger. Oh, God, give me strength—also guide, oh, guide me, Thou Great Jehovah. I shut the draught to my stove, set to gather my papers, and with pocket handkerchiefs dress myself in my warmest garments, and with a good-bye-look at my sacred emblems, pass out from my home in haste, hoping to reach the homestead before brother would perhaps be asleep. I wake my brother and tell him my warning—he reels. I hold him up. "Faint not in this awful hour! but hasten with me to East Brookfield." We reach there—and while the sleigh is being made ready to convey E. R. Hill to Worcester, my brother says: "What is going to become of me?" I said: "Moses, I shall put these papers and book account into H. W. King, Esq.'s hands. That sheriff's sale will be stopped, as I have this day accomplished that, and King will stop proceedings. By having this writ of review served on Deland before that 10 A.M., 26th of Feb., 1881 (that sheriff sale of the homestead was thus stayed), and do the best you can. Take out my daily newspapers from P.O., and see to my property with Mr. Haston. Good-bye! good-bye!" 12 midnight.—M. stands and looks at his sister leaving East Brookfield, the wife of the man wrapping her thick circular about me, placing hot stones at my feet. The husband takes the reins. We are wrapped close, for it is cold. The husband says: "Good night, Tyler. Keep up good spirit. We have the whip row of those devils. Wife, I shall get home by noon to-morrow." We reach Worcester, stopping at Mrs. E. Peck and Holbrook's, No. 10 Pearl street, 3 A.M.

About 10 A.M. I sent messenger for H. W. King, Esq., to come and see me, giving him my brother's book account against Flynn and Green, and papers telling him to serve that writ of review before that sale, etc., etc., and sending my keys of my house and all therein to Mr. Haston, with writing what to do, telling them how I was driven from my sacred home by conspirators who were going to take my liberty—far worse than murder! And I believe those men will yet be ranked in history co-equals with midnight assassins, highway robbers, and pirates of the seas. I leave Worcester at 5 P.M., Feb. 15, and Elizabeth R.

Hill's name is registered at Grand Union Hotel, New York, at 11 o'clock P.M. Thus for my liberty I am driven by malignant conspirators into another State, paying one dollar per day for room, besides cost of board and other incidentals. Thus shut out of my nice home, full of comforts, I demand that those men be dealt with as conspirators, and compelled to restore me my money for my great expenses and other losses more than hundred fold, and that they be hereafter compelled to keep the peace towards E. R. Hill, that she may in safety occupy and enjoy her legal citizen's rights and property in North Brookfield, Brookfield, Mass.

I wrote home, first of May, for two trunks to be filled and forwarded to Elizabeth R. Hill, Grand Central Depot, N. Y., by freight; keys to be sent by letter. My keys came on the 3d instant. A way-bill I at *last* found at Pier 25, on the 7th instant. No trunks! I wrote twice to East Brookfield, Mass., depot agent, to send me way-bill, and if those trunks were forwarded as I ordered? No reply. I wrote to my brother and Mr. Haston, on the 10th instant. Haston went to East Brookfield to see that Superintendent that S. told him "I had got my trunks. She will make a fuss—she's got her trunks!"

GENERAL OFFICE NEW HAVEN STEAMERS, }
     Piers 25 and 26 E. R., }

NEW YORK, May 13, 1881.

MADAM—We have not yet succeeded in finding your trunks, but expect to hear from them this afternoon.

Yours truly,

WM. SCOTT, Agent.

MRS. E. R. HILL, Grand Union Hotel,

    4th Avenue and 42d St., City.

Reader, I found my trunks on the 13th instant at Pier 25, with not one label on either trunk to tell whose, what, or where !!! The super said they came thus. I said: "Why did they come here? Why did not those trunks go to Ohio, Maine, or Virginia? My leather trunk had been broken open—the upper part of the lock in the bottom of the trunk, and all therein in mash jam!—many articles covered with road dirt, and many articles they wrote me were sent therein gone! Both trunks were strapped very tight.

Not hearing from E. Brookfield, only the above lie is circumstantial proof my trunks' labels were scratched off and ransacked at E. B. or its vicinity. For T. C. Bates rules, and he evidently means to keep Mrs. Hill in some trouble till they kill her. I have paid thousands of dollars car fare, and never had any trouble in my travels with baggage, but always had the very kindest of attention till since 1876. T. C. Bates and his contemporaries have been the cause of all ill-treatment and trouble with baggage in my travel on cars within their various forwarding custody. B. M. Nye told me in 1877, as we met on R. R. track in N. B., "that the R. R. Co. weren't agoing to let me walk on that track without paying," and he meant it. I told him my property was the sinking fund; that "that R. R. track was laid on to give you, the title president free rides," and build up the few arbitors of said R. R. T. C. Bates has got to be State R. R director. Has our R. R. corporation got to have such men rule in future? If so, let out the bank robbers from prison, and give them back their positions. But I say no! Stop Bates, Blackmer, Barnes, Nye, Tyler, and others, and give them their just merits with Pond and his contemporaries!

There was an "Act" passed in Mass. Legislature in 1878 said by Bates and his contemporaries, giving constables power to seize and put in lock-up (whoever they wish, I suppose); then, afterwards, take out warrant against their captive!!! Was not that "Act" passed purposely to cover those Cons., who had committed that crime many times in North Brookfield, Mass., before that heinous Act had birth? Again, in 1880, that (had it not ought to be called Salem witchcraft) Mass. Legislature passed an Act more diabolical than any Act upon Constitutional Records? was this most inhuman Act made to cover G. H. De Bevoise, B. Nye, T. C. Bates, W. Tyler, Oramel Martin's illegal perjury, malicious false imprisonment of Elizabeth R. Hill, Jan. 5, 1878? And thus to enable those men and others in their likeness hereafter to have law at their command to seize the body and bring into contumely and prison any one who may displease or in any way question their doings or sayings.

AN ACT concerning the Commitment and Transfer of Lunatics.

Be it enacted, &c., as follows:

SEC. 1. Whenever an application for the commitment of an alleged lunatic or insane person to any lunatic hospital or asylum shall be made, accompanied with the statement of the applicant required by law, the judge or justice having jurisdiction in the premises may thereupon, and after hearing such other evidence as he may deem proper, issue a warrant for the apprehension and bringing before him of the alleged lunatic or insane person, if, in the judgment of such judge or justice, the condition or conduct of such person seems to render it necessary or proper to do so for the safety of such person, or for due examination and hearing in the premises. Such warrant may be directed to and be served by a private person named in said warrant, as well as a qualified officer; and pending examination and hearing such order may be made concerning the care, custody, or confinement of such alleged lunatic or insane person as the judge or justice shall see fit.

SEC. 3. The fees of the judge or justice shall be as follows: For hearing and determining the application and filing papers, in cases where the alleged lunatic is brought before him, three dollars.

SEC. 7. This act shall take effect upon its passage. [*Approved April* 24, 1880.]

The time has arrived when the above inquisitors have "their law" now to dispose of Mrs. E. R. Hill, and thereby she will be heard of no more; and like a lightning flash we will consign her to oblivion. But Almighty God sent the bolt, thus warning the victim to escape the killing flash. There are, *I know, judges, lawyers, and men* who are in God's image in Mass. I appeal to you, gentlemen, to have those two heinous "Acts" above mentioned repealed the next legislature; and F. T. Blackmer, Esq., Worc.; L. E. Barnes and W. Tyler, N. B., punished as their perjury and vicious purpose against E. R. H., merits. The State ought now to agitate against those Acts from center to circumference. And may Almighty God give ear and revolutionize those laws, is the agonizing prayer of Elizabeth R. Hill, who has for her liberty been driven from her sacred cozy home at 42 Elm Street, North Brookfield, Mass., and thus enable me to return in safety to my home comforts and joys, and there, hereafter be protected from those trespassing conspirators.

In truth and sincerity I remain, yours

ELIZABETH R. HILL,

At Grand Union Hotel, 42d St. and 4th Ave.,

New York, N. Y.

www.ingramcontent.com/pod-product-compliance
Lightning Source LLC
Chambersburg PA
CBHW021426090426
42742CB00009B/1281